Illustration by Artem Vovchenko.

Algorithmic Investing

Iurii Vovchenko
Eric Brierley

2025
Second Edition

TABLE OF CONTENTS

1
WHAT IS ALGORITHMIC INVESTING?

The world of investing can be overwhelming at times. One of the most difficult challenges investors are faced with is trying to uncover practical insights from the abundance of data that is available to them. 50 years ago, investing was very different. You had to contact a company's investor relations department and wait a few weeks to obtain a copy of their annual report. You would read stock quotes from the newspaper, and the majority of the trades were taking place on the major stock exchanges run by humans. Today, we have instant access to all of a company's historical filings, financial data is presented to us in a user-friendly format across the internet free of cost; that includes financial ratios, valuation metrics, and stock prices that update in real-time, while the majority of trading activity is done by computers.

Things have changed. However, timeless investing principles remain true. The goal of this book is to show to you how you can utilize modern technology more effectively in your own personal investing decisions so you can grow your wealth long term. It's something we call algorithmic investing, contrary to algorithmic trading which would be a subject for another book.

Having read many of the most prominent books on investing myself, there seems to be an abundance of books on the theoretical and "mindset" side of investing. While those are certainly worth diving into, one can only be told to try and find "mispriced bets" and to invest with a "margin of safety" so many times. More serious investors want practical examples that they can learn from and to also acquire new knowledge and skills that can improve their investing results down the road. This book aims to teach you technical skills that allow you to make sense of the abundance of data available to us investors.

Why should I learn algorithmic investing?

At this point, you may be thinking that all this stuff sounds very complicated. It also sounds very time-consuming, and you are already short of time as it is. Perhaps you've never written a line of code in your life and have never viewed yourself as a coder. The goal of this book is not to turn you into a technology professional, it's to show you the many ways in which algorithmic investing can be used to save you time, simplify your own personal investing, and even reveal insights that no one else is looking at. If that sounds exciting to you, then you're in the right place.

Why does algorithmic value investing matter?

Investing is a competition. We are all competing for market-beating returns, and there's only so many companies out there that are trading at cheap enough prices to deliver those. And the competition is steep, we're up against professional fund managers with vast resources, years of experience, well-established networks, all designed to give them the best information. Retail investors, however, have certain advantages that fund managers don't have. Namely, the ability to invest their own money and not be obligated to obtain buy-in from your clients for each investment idea in order to retain them and stay in business. This book is written for the retail investor and aims to give them the knowledge required to be more competitive in the investing world.

In order to achieve this, we need to have access to the best possible information. We also need to know how to parse through information so we don't utilize faulty or irrelevant data in our decision making. In order to have the best information, we need to make use of modern tools that enable us to efficiently parse through vast amounts of data, and help us answer questions and learn new things.

One key application of algorithmic investing is its use in backtesting. Some well-known investors have used this to discover an investment strategy that has historically outperformed the market. In Joel Greenblatt's famous book The Little Book That Beats The Market, he shows us a very simple strategy that only uses two metrics (earnings yield and return on capital), and ranks every US stock based on those two metrics, then generates a list of 30-50 stocks that are at the top of this list. He states in the book that if you had bought every stock in that list, held them for a year, then re-ran the list again and sold the stocks no longer on the list and bought the stocks that are now on the list, you would have beaten the market. It was algorithmic investing that allowed him to uncover this strategy. It started with a simple idea, that stocks with high returns on capital (I.e., they make a lot of money relative to the capital invested in the business) that are selling at cheap prices (I.e., high earnings yields) should perform better than a broad market index.

Learning algorithmic investing allows you to be more scientific and intentional about your investing. You can use your creativity and critical thinking skills to develop a hypothesis, and then put it to the test to see what the results say. This is just one application of algorithmic investing, let me take you through another one to get you thinking about the possibilities.

A practical example

I spoke at the beginning of this chapter about being practical in this book. So let me be practical and show you a real example of how I used algorithmic value investing for my own personal advantage.

Recently, I got interested in bank stocks. Bank stocks tend to benefit from a rising interest rate environment due to their net interest margin (this is the total interest income they receive on their loans, less the interest they pay to acquire funding, divided by their total loans outstanding). As interest rates rise, banks can earn a higher interest rate on their loans, and these rates usually increase faster than the interest rates paid to acquire funding (such as interest rates on savings accounts). However, banks don't only earn income in the form of net interest income, they also earn non-interest income, which can consist of items such as account fees, service fees, dividends, as well as unrealized capital gains (unrealized meaning they have not sold the investment to realize the gain yet). Accounting standards require that certain investments be carried at their fair value, and be revalued every reporting period (usually every quarter). So if the investment has increased in value, it is recognized as income, even if the investment hasn't been sold yet.

When interest rates are rising, this can sometimes lead to equity prices falling, which would mean the bank is recognizing unrealized losses, and may even have negative non-interest income. So there are two counteracting forces at play for bank stocks in a rising interest rate environment. Because of this, my goal was to understand how each bank derives their revenue from each source, so I created a script which tells me exactly that.

Below is the table that is generated by such a script. I also filtered out any non-US stock, and kept the industry limited to regional (smaller) banks. You can see the columns include market capitalization, Price/Earnings ratio, Non-Interest Income as a % of revenue MRQ (most recent quarter), Net Interest Income as a % of revenue MRQ, and 3 year averages of Non-Interest Income and Net Interest Income as a % of revenue.

Table Name

BankStocksRevenueBreakdown

Name	MarketCap	PE Ratio	NonInterestIncome% (mrq)	NetInterestIncome% (mrq)	NonInterestIncome% (3 Year Avg)	NetInterestIncome% (3 Year Avg)
US BANCORP DE/Banks-Regional@Financial Services	50446.45	8.6797	0.3871	0.6129	0.4436	0.5554
PNC FINANCIAL SERVICES GROUP INC /Banks-Regional@Financial Ser...	49611.72	5.4901	0.347	0.653	0.4090	0.5902
TRUST FINANCIAL CORP/Banks-Regional@Financial Services	40547.8942	6.3674	0.346	0.654	0.4094	0.5906
M&T BANK CORP/Banks-Regional@Financial Services	20923.6608	10.5056	0.2336	0.7664	0.3204	0.6796
FIFTH THIRD BANCORP/Banks-Regional@Financial Services	17403.4234	7.1151	0.2926	0.7074	0.4034	0.5966
REGIONS FINANCIAL CORP/Banks-Regional@Financial Services	16709.26	7.4689	0.3046	0.6954	0.3623	0.6677
CITIZENS FINANCIAL GROUP INC /CR/Banks-Regional@Financial Services	16043.4756	7.6452	0.2262	0.7738	0.2992	0.7008
HUNTINGTON BANCSHARES INC /MD/Banks-Regional@Financial Services	14921.3235	6.5315	0.2501	0.7499	0.3382	0.6618
KEYCORP /NEW/Banks-Regional@Financial Services	10761.2373	5.4918	0.3699	0.6301	0.4077	0.5923
FIRST HORIZON CORP/Banks-Regional@Financial Services	8014.4808	7.3393	0.2408	0.7592	0.3921	0.6079
COMMERCE BANCSHARES INC /MO/Banks-Regional@Financial Services	7267.477	14.6139	0.3386	0.6614	0.3734	0.6266
CULLEN/FROST BANKERS INC /Banks-Regional@Financial Services	6959.6523	12.017	0.1301	0.8699	0.2715	0.7285
WEBSTER FINANCIAL CORP/Banks-Regional@Financial Services	6654.0659	12.516	0.1592	0.8408	0.2291	0.7709
SVB FINANCIAL GROUP/Banks-Regional@Financial Services	6311.0305	4.1823	0.2333	0.7667	0.447	0.553
BOK FINANCIAL CORP/Banks-Regional@Financial Services	5799.2073	10.6983	0.273	0.727	0.3974	0.6026
SouthState Corp/Banks-Regional@Financial Services	5730.8354	11.3376	0.1812	0.8188	0.239	0.761
COMERICA INC /NEW/Banks-Regional@Financial Services	5708.8454	4.8095	0.2563	0.7437	0.3338	0.6662

Instead of having to look into each bank, and calculate these figures individually, I can create a script to generate this information, along with any other information I may also find useful. And by looking at this data I can quickly get an ad-hoc snapshot into the US banking industry and understand how banks derive their revenue and get a sense of how exposed each bank is to changes in interest rates. What's even better is this script is dynamic, meaning it always updates with the latest quarterly data whenever I choose to run it in the future. It only took about 10 minutes to create the script and the code is not more complicated than the formulae you would use in Microsoft Excel.

Hopefully, from this example you can start to visualize the possibilities. Here are a few more examples of insights we can obtain via scripting:

- Show me a list of companies that have experienced annual revenue growth at least twice that of their industry (over the past 5 years).

- Create a chart that shows me the total capital expenditure made by oil and gas companies by quarter going back 10 years.

- Rank every stock on the 3 following metrics: operating margin, debt-to-equity ratio, and Price/Earnings ratio, and show me a list of the 10 highest-ranking stocks.

- Calculate a firm's cost of capital using the most recent quarterly financial and interest rate data available.

- Show me a list of companies that have grown their revenue at least twice as much as their industry competitors over the past 5 years.

With just a rudimentary knowledge of basic coding, you can use your creativity to obtain unique insights into the market that perhaps no one else has identified.

2

VALUE INVESTING VS TECHNICAL ANALYSIS

Charlie Munger is famously quoted saying "all intelligent investing is value investing". It seems that when people immerse themselves in the world of investing, they fall into one of two categories: value investors or growth investors. Value investors believe the goal of investing is to buy a dollar for fifty cents or less and to not be swayed by your emotions towards a particular company; and rely on cold hard calculation. This often leads value investors to place an emphasis on objective, numbers-based analysis such as financial ratios, valuation metrics, historical growth trends, and the like. Growth investors believe your focus should be on building sizable positions in high quality businesses with strong future growth prospects. If this requires paying a premium, then so be it, it will work out in the end because investing in high quality businesses is the best long-term wealth accumulation method. This approach tends to lead investors to place a greater emphasis on qualitative characteristics while potentially ignoring a valuation that is objectively detached from reality. I think the truth lies somewhere in the middle.

Value investors are correct in their pursuit of undervalued companies, but a sole focus on quantitative characteristics may lead you into value traps (buying a company for the sake of its apparent undervaluation while ignoring recognizable pitfalls). Growth investors are correct in their emphasis on qualitative characteristics and trying to assess a business's future potential. Over time, we've seen a notable shift in business assets from tangible (equipment, inventory, land, property) to intangible (technical expertise, brand names, intellectual property). A study conducted by consulting firm Ocean Tomo shows that in the year 1975, 83% of business assets owned by S&P 500 companies were tangible while 17% were intangible. In the year 2020, this has shifted to 90% intangible and 10% tangible.

The implication of this is that the intangible aspects of businesses have more influence on valuation now than ever before, and this will likely continue to be the case in the future.

At the core of value investing is formulating a hypothesis about what a given company's future may look like, valuing a company based on that future, comparing that back to its current price, and taking advantage of any discrepancies. It requires you to be a contrarian and it requires you to be right. To do this, understanding how valuation works is paramount. To help with this, I have put together an illustrative exercise that can help you think about valuation (whether you're a seasoned investor, or a beginner).

Let's say there is a business and all that business owns is a bank account with $100M in cash. It has no debts, no operations and no employees. How much is a business like that worth? Obviously, $100M. Anything less or more than that would be illogical. Now let's take it one step further…

Let's say that the same business also has a loan from a bank for $30M. How much is that business worth now? Because that business could be bought, the debt paid off in its entirety, and the remaining cash paid back to its owners, it's worth $70M.

Now let's say that same business also owns $30M worth of inventory. How much is that business worth now? Things get a little more complicated here because accounting standards come into play. Businesses must value inventory at the lower of cost (what they paid to acquire that inventory) and net realizable value (what they can sell it for). Therefore, if a business can sell inventory for more than it costs them to purchase it, this inventory may be worth more than $40M. This creates some uncertainty, because in order to determine what the business is worth, we would have to know the exact amount the business could make selling that inventory, and this would require knowledge of the industry, the customers, the competition, etc.

So far we have just dealt with balance-sheet based methods of valuation. Meaning everything just described was either an asset or a liability. This is relatively straightforward to value because we just need to calculate a sum of the values of the assets, subtract the values of the liabilities and we can arrive at a valuation. But what if this business has ongoing operations?

Let's say this business wants to begin selling physical items. To do this they must purchase equipment that costs $15M, hire employees in manufacturing, administrative, marketing, and management roles which will cost $7.5M annually, and purchase $30M worth of raw materials inventory (we can call this inventory purchase a working capital investment) . These new factors add much more complexity to the valuation and raise the following questions:

- How much can the inventory be sold for?
- Will the business be able to sell that inventory for enough money such that they can pay all their employee's wages?
- How much inventory will the business buy next year?
- Will this business expand their operations in the future?
- How many years will they continue to operate for?
- How much depreciation should be charged against their equipment? What can the equipment be sold for in the future?
- How much interest must be paid on the bank loan?
- What discount rate should we use for the future cash flows?

Let's assume the business can sell the inventory for $60M, so a 200% markup. Then for each of the next 5 years, they will purchase another $30M of inventory, plus an additional $5M (so $35M in year 2, $40M in year 3, and so on) and sell it at a 200% markup as well. At the end of the fifth year, the business will sell off all its assets (including the $15M in equipment). The equipment will be depreciated using the straight-line method, with a 5 year useful life and a $5M salvage value. Meaning the annual depreciation expense is $2M [($15M cost - $5M salvage value)/5 years = $2M per year]. This business also has a cost of capital of 10%.

	Year 1	Year 2	Year 3	Year 4	Year 5
Revenue	$60,000,000	$70,000,000	$80,000,000	$90,000,000	$100,000,000
Cost of Goods Sold	$30,000,000	$35,000,000	$40,000,000	$45,000,000	$50,000,000
Gross Profit	$30,000,000	$35,000,000	$40,000,000	$45,000,000	$50,000,000
Employee Wages	$7,500,000	$7,500,000	$7,500,000	$7,500,000	$7,500,000
Depreciation Expense	$2,000,000	$2,000,000	$2,000,000	$2,000,000	$2,000,000
Operating Income	$20,500,000	$25,500,000	$30,500,000	$35,500,000	$40,500,000
Less: Working Capital Increase	$5,000,000	$5,000,000	$5,000,000	$5,000,000	
Less: Capital Expenditures	$15,000,000				-$5,000,000
Add: Depreciation	$2,000,000	$2,000,000	$2,000,000	$2,000,000	$2,000,000
Free Cash Flow (to Firm)	$2,500,000	$22,500,000	$27,500,000	$32,500,000	$47,500,000
Present Value (Discounted @ 10%)	$2,272,727	$18,595,041	$20,661,157	$22,197,937	$29,493,763
Enterprise Value (Sum of Discounted FCFF)	$93,220,626				
Less: Bank Loan	-$30,000,000				
Add: Cash Balance	$100,000,000				
Equity Value	$163,220,626				

As we can see, under those conditions the business's equity value is just over $163M. Because we have perfect knowledge of what the future holds, we can make an accurate valuation. However, in the real world, we do not have such information, and our goal is to get as close to perfect information as we reasonably can. It also goes to show that as soon as we introduced ongoing operations for this hypothetical business, the valuation got much more complicated.

Businesses with futures that are more uncertain and more difficult to predict are more prone to valuation discrepancies because investors may hold very different opinions on what their futures will look like. It also means that their stock prices are more volatile, as any unexpected news that comes out about the company could drastically alter investors' perceptions of their future success. There is more room for upside, but also more room for downside. Contrast this with a company that is much more predictable, such as an established railroad business. We could safely assume that the next year's revenues will be roughly equal to the current year's revenues, plus or minus some modest growth or decline. Expenses will probably stay in line with what they have been in the past, as will working capital investments, capital expenditures, depreciation, etc. A Business like this will have far less sudden swings in stock price, have far less downside risk, but also less upside potential. Most investors can accurately predict what their future will look like.

This is the game that value investors play. And by marrying the qualitative, "story" element of a business with a calculated, quantitative approach, we can build assumptions on what the future may hold.

So What About Technical Analysis?

I will not go into a religious war between value investors and technical analysis pros, but I need to say a few words about technical analysis because it is used by many investors out there. I will give a short introduction to this subject so you would have a good overview of what is available out there. Please, note I do not use it personally.

The main idea behind technical analysis is that the stock price follows certain patterns, and it is the responsibility of an investor to recognize those patterns and use that for future price prediction. Usually, technical analysis pros love to use the so-called candle-stick charts. Here is an example of such a chart:

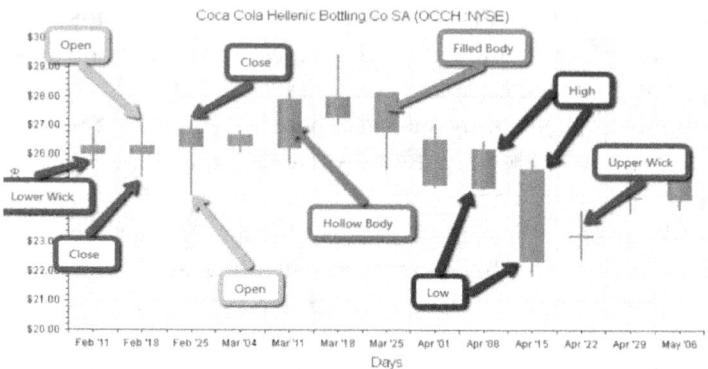

The red color signals that the stock price has fallen on that specific day and the green means the stock price has risen. The thick part(the candle) shows open and close prices and the thin part(the wick) shows the min and max prices that day.

The technical analysis pros identified dozens of patterns with creative names such as trigger line put, neck line, head and shoulders, falling wedge, etc. Here is an example of the falling wedge pattern:

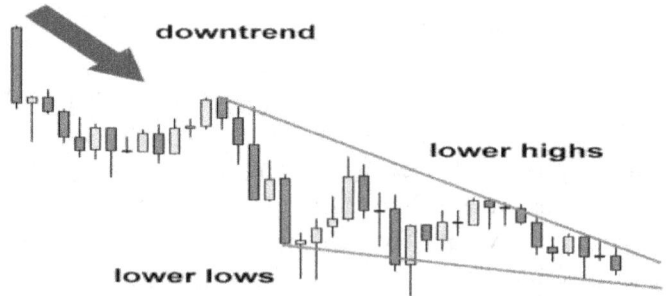

The idea is that it gets narrower with lower highs at the end of the wedge. So somewhere at the end might be a good idea to act and do a purchase at the end of the wedge. The reasoning usually is as follows: since the price refuses to break the lower level of support, selling pressure gradually decreases, the upper level of resistance is broken, and the price breaks out and begins a strong upward trend. If it sounds like astrology for stock trading then yes it does...

Technical analysis pros also love to draw the lines of price "support". These are imaginary lines drawn at a certain price level of the stock through which it refuses to break through multiple times, likely because there is a certain number of investors that refuse to sell at such a low price. They might be onto something here, possibly it is a psychological thing, but since I am "a science believer" and I would need a good solid mathematical theory behind these patterns. So I am not convinced Technical Analysis is a thing.

It is up to the readers to decide if they want to incorporate Technical Analysis into their algorithms. Here is a sneak peek at the candle-stick price data API in Tickernomics (we will learn more about scripting in later chapters):

GetPrice(ticker,int day, string propName) retrieve company stock price at the specific day(-1 for latest price). propName can be empty string or one of these: PriceClose,PriceOpenRaw, PriceCloseRaw, PriceHighRaw, PriceLowRaw, PriceVolume

3

ACCOUNTING BASICS

Before we go any further, it's important to discuss some fundamental finance and accounting concepts to ensure all readers of this book can understand the ideas we present in this book later. This chapter is meant to establish the baseline level of technical knowledge that readers must be equipped with before we dive into the coding side of things. This section may cover some concepts that you are already familiar with. However, I hope you can use this chapter as a way to review some concepts that you may already know, or if these are completely new to you then it can educate you. We will discuss topics such as financial accounting, management decision making, capital allocation, risk and reward trade-offs, asset pricing models, and factor investing.

Basic Financial Accounting - The Income Statement

Accounting is the language of business. It's the way businesses communicate their financial performance to a broader audience. Accounting standards, such as US GAAP (US Generally Accepted Accounting Principles, and IFRS (International Financial Reporting Standards) have been developed to form a set of standardized principles that all companies must comply with when reporting their financial results to financial statement readers. Think of reading financial results like ordering from McDonald's; regardless of which McDonald's you visit, when you order a Big Mac you know exactly what you're getting. Similar, when you read financial statements you know that all companies reported those results following the same rule book. The good news is that by law public companies are required to release financial statements regularly (usually quarterly). Value investors rely on these statements to accurately value businesses.

As an aside, if you ever see a company report "non-GAAP" financial metrics, it is because those metrics are not in compliance with the accounting standards, and they have been defined by the company's own creative will. This doesn't necessarily mean they're not useful and should be ignored, but ensure that the formula they used to define the metric is logical and consistent over time.

There are four main financial statements you will find, and they are connected to each other in different ways. The first financial statement that can be prepared by a company is the income statement.

Shopify Inc.
Consolidated Statements of Operations and Comprehensive (Loss) Income
Expressed in US $000's, except share and per share amounts

	Note	Years December 31, 2022 $
Revenues		
Subscription solutions	23	1,487,759
Merchant solutions	23	4,112,105
		5,599,864
Cost of revenues		
Subscription solutions		330,867
Merchant solutions		2,514,878
		2,845,745
Gross profit		2,754,119
Operating expenses		
Sales and marketing		1,230,490
Research and development		1,503,234
General and administrative	10, 17	707,765
Transaction and loan losses		134,929
Total operating expenses		3,576,418
(Loss) income from operations		(822,299)
Other (expense) income, net		
Interest income		79,141
Interest expense	15	(3,499)
Net realized gain on equity and other investments	5	124,006
Net unrealized (loss) gain on equity and other investments	5	(2,998,296)
Foreign exchange (loss) gain		(1,901)
Total other (expense) income, net		(2,800,549)
(Loss) income before income taxes		(3,622,848)
Recovery of (provision for) income taxes	21	162,430
Net (loss) income		(3,460,418)

The income statement states a company's revenues at the top, then it states a company's cost of goods sold (or cost of revenues). Total revenues minus cost of revenues gives you gross profit. Next, operating expenses are listed. This includes items like selling, general & administrative expenses, research and development, marketing expenses, and any other expense that is necessary for a company to run its operations. Gross profit minus operating expenses gives us operating income. As we saw in the previous chapter, operating income is a critically important metric to understanding any business since it tells us how much income a company has made purely from its operations. Companies with high operating profitability relative to industry peers likely have a unique competitive advantage, which makes their business special, so it should not be ignored. Thus if the goal is to assess a company's operating effectiveness relative to peers, then using operating income is useful.

Underneath operating income we have other incomes and expenses. These are separated out of operating income because these items tend to be one-off items, or items related to interest income and expenses. Interest expense, while it is a legitimate expense, is one that is influenced by changes to interest rates set by central banks as opposed to a company's operations. Interest rates can also change because of other factors, for example, a more financially stable company will be quoted a lower interest rate on their debt.

Additionally, as we can see in Shopify's income statement above, they own investments in other entities that are subject to change in value. Certain investments are required by accounting rules to be revalued at each reporting period (I.e., each quarter for a public company) so if those investments lose value, then that is reported as a loss on the income statement and it's called an *unrealized* loss. But such a gain or a loss does not relate to a company's operations. Although such a gain or loss should never be ignored, since it does still influence a business's value, when assessing operating effectiveness it's best to keep those items separate. Other items you may find in this "Other expenses/incomes" section can be things like foreign exchange gains/losses, changes to pension plan liabilities, goodwill impairment write-offs, and more.

Once we have adjusted for these other incomes/expenses, we arrive at net income before taxes. We then deduct the income tax expense/benefit to arrive at net income. Typically, if a company reports a profit, they have to pay taxes, and if a company reports a loss, they report an income tax "benefit". However, income for accounting purposes is not the same thing as income for tax purposes, so this rule doesn't always hold true. In the Shopify example above, we can see that they reported an income tax benefit of $162MM, and a loss from operations of $822MM, so in this instance it does make sense that Shopify reported an income tax benefit. Shopify's *Loss before income taxes* was $3,622MM and much of this loss related to the unrealized losses on their investments, which are not included in the calculation of taxable income until they are sold.

That gives us a quick overview of the income statement. It's also important to understand that income, revenues, and expenses are all flow variables, meaning the values they represent are values that have accumulated over a period of time. In order to know what a company's revenue is, we need to also know what time period we are looking at, whether that is a year, a quarter, a month, etc.

Additionally, the income statement is prepared using accrual accounting. This means that revenues are recognized when earned, and expenses are recognized when incurred. For example, if a company that sells golf balls has a year-end date of December 31, and on December 30 they receive payment for an order for 100 golf balls, but they don't ship the golf balls until January 2, they cannot recognize the payment they received as revenue on their income statement for the period ending December 31. Once they have delivered the golf balls, then they can recognize revenue, but until that point it is recognized as "unearned" revenue (or deferred revenue) and it is a liability on the company's balance sheet (since they are liable for the delivery of the golf balls to the customer).

Similarly, with expenses, if a company's year-end date is December 31 and they pay their payroll on January 5, the portion of that payroll that relates to work performed from the previous payroll date until December 31 is recorded as an expense, even if the cash hasn't been paid to the employees yet.

Basic Financial Accounting - The Statement of Changes in Equity

The second financial statement that can be prepared is the statement of changes in equity. This is sometimes referred to as the *Statement of Retained Earnings* or the *Statement of Changes in Owners' Equity*.

Shopify Inc.
Consolidated Statements of Changes in Shareholders' Equity
Expressed in US $000's except share amounts

	Note	Common Stock		Additional Paid-In Capital $	Accumulated Other Comprehensive Income (Loss) $	(Accumulated Deficit) Retained Earnings $	Total $
		Shares[1]	Amount $				
As at December 31, 2020		1,225,288,710	6,115,232	261,436	8,770	15,285	6,400,723
Adjustment related to the adoption of ASU 2020-06, Debt		—	—	(158,810)	—	8,198	(150,612)
As at January 1, 2021		1,225,288,710	6,115,232	102,626	8,770	23,483	6,250,111
Exercise of stock options		14,948,400	166,057	(57,463)	—	—	108,594
Stock-based compensation		—	—	330,763	—	—	330,763
Vesting of restricted share units		6,934,480	214,852	(214,852)	—	—	—
Issuance of Class A subordinate voting shares, net of offering costs of $7,742, net of tax of $2,790	19	11,800,000	1,543,958	—	—	—	1,543,958
Net income and comprehensive income for the year		—	—	—	(14,744)	2,914,659	2,899,915
As at December 31, 2021		1,258,971,590	8,040,099	161,074	(5,974)	2,938,142	11,133,341
Exercise of stock options		3,126,869	34,815	(17,266)	—	—	17,549
Stock-based compensation		—	—	549,142	—	—	549,142
Vesting of restricted share units		7,380,507	470,524	(470,524)	—	—	—
Issuance of the Founder share		1	—	—	—	—	—
Issuance of shares related to business acquisitions	19, 24	5,649,600	201,994	(192,220)	—	—	9,774
Net loss and comprehensive loss for the year		—	—	—	(10,499)	(3,460,418)	(3,470,917)
As at December 31, 2022		1,275,128,567	8,747,432	30,206	(16,473)	(522,276)	8,238,889

[1] Prior year share amounts have been retrospectively adjusted to reflect the Share Split effected in June 2022. See Note 19 for details.

This financial statement can get pretty technical, but for now we still stick to the basics and also explain a few more complex topics to give you a flavor for what this financial statement is all about.

You will see a separate column in this financial statement for each account that is a part of equity. Let's start with Common Stock. This represents the total value of money received by the company for issuing common stock to shareholders. In the above example, the company breaks out that change in common shares as well as the change in the value of common stock dating back to December 31, 2020. We can see that Shopify's share count has increased for a number of reasons. Firstly, the issuance of Class A common shares - 11.8 million in 2021. Secondly, the exercise of stock options in each year. Because Shopify offers its employees an employee stock option plan as part of their compensation package, this will likely continue into the foreseeable future. We can also see there were common shares issued relating to *Vesting of restricted share units*, this also relates to Shopify's employee compensation package and is a type of share that only becomes a common share once certain conditions have been met. They usually have a vesting period associated with them which is a number of years an employee must stay with Shopify in order to earn the shares. Once that time period has passed, the restricted share units are "vested" and the employee now owns them. This will also likely continue into the foreseeable future.

We can also observe that in 2022, there were 5,649,600 shares issued relating to business acquisitions. This is likely part of Shopify's corporate strategy, and companies can either use internally generated cash flow from operations to fund a business acquisition, or use some combination of debt or shares issued. Because Shopify's total share count has increased, we refer to this as *dilution*. Because a shareholder of Shopify in 2020 now owns a smaller percentage of the company compared to 2022 because more shares have been issued, thus the shareholder has been *diluted*. It is always important to understand whether a company's share count is increasing or decreasing as this will certainly influence your investment.

The next item is *Additional Paid-In Capital ("APIC")*. This item refers to the amounts of money paid by an investor for shares of stock in excess of par value. The par value of common stock is usually very low ($0.01 most of the time), and some jurisdictions even allow for "no par" common stock to be issued. Companies that issue no par common stock will usually have Common Stock balances much higher than APIC balances on their statement of changes in equity.

The final column is *(Accumulated Deficit)/Retained Earnings*. If this figure is positive it is called retained earnings, if it is negative it is called accumulated deficit. This figure can be interpreted as the total amount of earnings a company has earned throughout their history, minus any cash distributions paid to shareholders such as dividends. For a given period, it is calculated as the balance as of the ending of the prior period, plus a company's net income or net loss during the period, minus any dividends paid to shareholders.

Similar to this in the *Accumulated Other Comprehensive Income/Loss* (also known as "AOCI") account. However, this account is only for certain income statement items that are not included in net income due to the accounting rules surrounding them. This topic of accounting can get quite complex and is outside the scope of this book, but for now just note that AOCI is a separate section certain income statement items can be reported in.

I.e., Common Stock (that total value of money the business received for issuing common stock to shareholders, Additional Paid-In Capital, Accumulated Other Comprehensive Loss, and Retained Earnings/Accumulated Deficit (the total amount of

Basic Financial Accounting - The Balance Sheet

The third financial statement that can be prepared by a company is the balance sheet, also known as the *statement of financial position.* The balance sheet consists of stock variables, meaning the numbers you see represent values at a given point in time. This is in contrast to the income statement which has flow variables. For example, "$100M USD in Total Assets on a Balance Sheet on 1st of May", means a company had exactly 100M USD of Total Assets specifically **on** 1st of May. This is in contrast to Income Statement, where for example "$50M in Total Revenue for Q3 of 2022" would mean a company had $50M in Total Revenues accumulated **during** Q3 of 2022.

Shopify Inc.
Consolidated Balance Sheets
Expressed in US $000's except share amounts

	Note	As at December 31, 2022 $	As at December 31, 2021 $
Assets			
Current assets			
Cash and cash equivalents	4	1,649,328	2,502,992
Marketable securities	5	3,403,622	5,265,101
Trade and other receivables, net	6	273,055	192,209
Merchant cash advances, loans and related receivables, net	7	580,114	470,722
Income taxes receivable	21	4,695	5,023
Other current assets	8	139,659	103,273
		6,050,473	8,539,320
Long-term assets			
Property and equipment, net	9	130,821	105,526
Right-of-use assets, net	10	355,145	196,388
Intangible assets, net	11	390,148	138,496
Deferred tax assets	21	40,822	48,369
Equity and other investments ($868,960 and $3,412,366, carried at fair value)	5	1,953,460	3,955,545
Goodwill	12	1,836,282	356,528
		4,706,678	4,800,852
Total assets		10,757,151	13,340,172
Liabilities and shareholders' equity			
Current liabilities			
Accounts payable and accrued liabilities	13	532,569	456,688
Income taxes payable	21	9,390	13,505
Deferred revenue	14	295,888	216,792
Lease liabilities	10	18,161	15,748
		856,008	702,733
Long-term liabilities			
Deferred revenue	14	267,513	162,932
Lease liabilities	10	465,135	246,776
Convertible senior notes	15	913,312	910,963
Deferred tax liabilities	21	16,294	183,427
		1,662,254	1,504,098
Commitments and contingencies	10, 17		
Shareholders' equity			
Common stock, unlimited Class A subordinate voting shares authorized, 1,195,697,614 and 1,139,544,920, issued and outstanding, unlimited Class B restricted voting shares authorized, 79,430,952 and 119,426,670 issued and outstanding, 1 Founder share authorized, 1 and nil issued and outstanding [1][2]	19	8,747,432	8,040,099
Additional paid-in capital		30,206	161,074
Accumulated other comprehensive loss	20	(16,473)	(5,974)
(Accumulated deficit) retained earnings		(522,276)	2,938,142
Total shareholders' equity		8,238,889	11,133,341
Total liabilities and shareholders' equity		10,757,151	13,340,172

The balance sheet starts by listing out a company's assets. *Current assets* represent assets that are expected to be converted into cash within 1 year or less, such as short term investments, receivables, and inventory. Assets are typically listed from top to bottom in order of liquidity (i.e., how easily that asset can be converted into cash), with cash at the top and something non-liquid like goodwill at the bottom. *Non-current assets* are assets that the company does not expect to convert into cash within the next year, this includes items like property, plant and equipment ("PPE"), intangible assets, goodwill, and long term investments.

Liabilities are reported underneath assets, and similar to assets, they are listed in order of liquidity. Current liabilities are liabilities that are expected to be settled within the next year or less, such as accounts payable, accrued expenses, incomes taxes payable, etc. Long term liabilities are those that are expected to be settled in over one year, such as long term debt, lease obligations, deferred tax liabilities, etc.

Underneath liabilities is shareholders' equity, which includes the items present on the statement of changes in equity which we previously discussed.

Basic Financial Accounting - The Statement of Cash Flows

The final financial statement that a company usually prepares is the statement of cash flows.

	Note	Years ended	
		December 31, 2022 $	December 31, 2021 $
Cash flows from operating activities			
Net (loss) income for the year		(3,460,418)	2,914,659
Adjustments to reconcile net (loss) income to net cash (used in) provided by operating activities:			
Amortization and depreciation		90,520	66,308
Stock-based compensation	19	549,142	330,763
Amortization of debt offering costs	15	2,349	2,343
Impairment of right-of-use assets and leasehold improvements	9, 10	84,314	30,145
Provision for transaction and loan losses		73,604	43,781
Deferred income tax (recovery) expense	21	(186,571)	190,963
Revenue related to non-cash consideration	14	(121,503)	(58,380)
Net loss (gain) on equity and other investments	5	2,918,684	(2,859,800)
Unrealized foreign exchange loss		11,702	4,570
Changes in operating assets and liabilities:			
Trade and other receivables		(104,527)	(72,300)
Merchant cash advances and related receivables [1]		(23,385)	(234,794)
Other current assets		(30,767)	(50,151)
Non-cash consideration received in exchange for services	5, 14	(273,201)	(268,058)
Accounts payable and accrued liabilities		36,541	138,175
Income taxes receivable and payable	21	(3,941)	45,263
Deferred revenue	14	305,180	309,289
Lease assets and liabilities		(4,175)	2,935
Net cash (used in) provided by operating activities		(136,448)	535,711
Cash flows from investing activities			
Purchase of marketable securities		(5,011,129)	(7,337,366)
Maturity of marketable securities		6,890,167	5,750,224
Purchases and originations of loans [1]		(525,538)	(198,523)
Repayments of loans [1]		366,855	167,240
Purchase of equity and other investments	5	(635,156)	(650,233)
Acquisitions of property and equipment		(50,018)	(50,788)
Acquisition of businesses, net of cash acquired	24	(1,753,748)	(59,627)
Net cash used in investing activities		(718,567)	(2,379,073)
Cash flows from financing activities			
Proceeds from public equity offerings, net of issuance costs	19	—	1,541,168
Proceeds from the exercise of stock options		17,349	108,594
Net cash provided by financing activities		17,349	1,649,762
Effect of foreign exchange on cash and cash equivalents		(16,198)	(7,005)
Net decrease in cash and cash equivalents		(853,664)	(200,605)
Cash and cash equivalents – Beginning of Year		2,502,992	2,703,597
Cash and cash equivalents – End of Year		1,649,328	2,502,992
Supplemental cash flow information:			
Cash paid for amounts included in the measurement of lease liabilities included in cash flows from operating activities		39,590	26,166
Lease liabilities arising from obtaining right-of-use assets		264,912	118,091
Acquired property and equipment remaining unpaid		10,594	8,052
Cash paid for (recovered from) income taxes, net		27,287	(30,466)
Cash paid for interest		1,150	1,287

There are three main sections of this financial statement: operating activities, investing activities, and financing activities. The point is to show the various inflows and outflows of cash to and from the company. The cash flow statement is arguably the most useful financial statement for assessing a company because cash is so important.

The operating activities section tells you how much a company earned in cash from the operations of its business. It starts with net income at the top, adds back any non-cash expenses that were recognized on the income statement (such as stock based compensation, depreciation and amortization, impairment of assets, etc.), then adds back any unrealized gains or losses, and finally adjusts for changes in the company's operating assets and liabilities. The reason the operating activities section adjusts for these items is because the income statement is prepared using accrual accounting, so not all revenues reported on the income statement have had their associated cash payment received by the company yet, and not all expenses have been paid for in cash. And because the point of the cash flow statement is to show the reader cash flows, we have to make such adjustments to convert net income into cash flow from operations.these items are adjusted for.

The next section is cash flows from investing activities. In this section, "investing" does not necessarily mean investing in securities - although a company's investments and sales of securities would be included here. It can also mean investments into property, plant and equipment (commonly called capital expenditures, or CAPEX), investments in the form of business acquisitions, and more.

The last section is the financing section. This section breaks out cash inflows and outflows related to financing the operations of the business such as proceeds received from issuing common shares, proceeds received from issuing debt, and more.

Now that we have a basic understanding of how companies present the results of their operations to investors, let's discuss how investors combine certain financial data to better understand a company.

There are hundreds of different financial ratios and metrics out there that investors use, we will not discuss every single one. However we will discuss a few important ones that also can serve as learning opportunities for how other ratios are devised.

Return on assets ("ROA") is a fairly common financial ratio that measures a company's net income relative to their total assets. It compares a flow variable (net income) to a stock variable (total assets). Because of this, it is important to take the average asset balance over the period the net income is calculated for. So if we are trying to calculate ROA for the 2022 full year, we take total assets as of the 2022 year-end, plus the total assets as of the 2021 year-end, and divide by 2 to get an average. Net income is then divided by this number to arrive at ROA. The same principle must be applied to any financial metric that compares a flow variable to a stock variable.

It is also important to only compare a company's ROA relative to industry peers, because an oil and gas refining company will have a very different ROA than a software company (software companies usually do not have a lot of assets), but that doesn't necessarily mean one is superior to the other.

Another class of financial ratios that is important to know are liquidity ratios. These measure a company's ability to pay its short term obligations, although they can also offer insight into a company's operating effectiveness. For example, the *Days Inventory Outstanding* ratio tells you how long, on average, it takes for a company to sell its inventory. It is calculated using the following formula:

(Average Inventory/Cost of Goods Sold) x 365

Similarly, *Days Sales Outstanding* is used to calculate how long, on average, it takes a company to collect payment for the sale of goods or services. And *Days Payables Outstanding* measures how long, on average, it takes a company to pay its suppliers. They are calculated using the following formulae:

Days Payables Outstanding = (Average Accounts Payable/Cost of Goods Sold) x 365

Days Sales Outstanding = (Average Accounts Receivable/Total Revenues) x 365

Here is an example of Coca-Cola's ($KO) liquidity ratios:

Liquidity Analysis	KO	Industry Avg
Current Ratio(mrq)	1.15	2.32
Quick Ratio(mrq)	0.79	1.71
Avg Receivables Collection(days)(ttm)	38.15	52.27
Avg Inventory Outstanding(days)(ttm)	79	140.51
Avg Payables Outstanding(days)(ttm)	184.06	171.84
Cash Conversion Cycle(ttm)	-66.9	20.94

The "Cash Conversion Cycle" is a unique metric that combines the 3 aforementioned liquidity ratios. It is calculated as follows:

Days Inventory Outstanding + Days Receivables Outstanding - Days Payables Outstanding

This formula measures how long it takes a company to sell its inventory, collect payment for the sale, and then pay back its suppliers. We can see that Coca-Cola has a negative cash conversion cycle, versus the industry average of 20.94 days. It's quite rare to see this, but what it means is that Coca-Cola can sell its inventory, collect payment, before it has to pay back its suppliers, so they never have to tie up any money to purchase inventory, and then pay their suppliers for that inventory, since they receive the cash for the sale of the inventory before they're required to pay their suppliers. This shows us how much market power Coca-Cola has that they are able to impose such lenient payment terms with their suppliers. For some companies a negative cash conversion cycle can be a sign of real liquidity issues if they are delaying payment to their suppliers, so this must always be analyzed taking the company's situation into account.

Another important class of financial ratios are solvency ratios.

Solvency Ratios	KO	Industry Avg
Debt/Equity Ratio(mrq)	2.59	1.91
Debt/Assets Ratio(mrq)	0.72	0.54
Equity/Assets Ratio(mrq)	0.28	0.46
EBIT/Interest(ttm)	11.22	8.85
EBITDA/Interest(ttm)	12.88	13.84

These ratios aim to measure a company's ability to continue to stay in business for the long term and cover its long term debts. Interest coverage ratios such as EBIT/Interest (earnings before interest and taxes), and EBITDA/Interest (earnings before interest, taxes, depreciation, and amortization) show how well a company can meet its interest payments. And ratios like Debt/Equity tell you how much debt versus equity a company has used to finance their assets. We can see above that Coca-Cola has used more debt than equity when compared to their industry peers (2.59 vs. 1.91). This is not necessarily a bad thing, especially considering their EBIT/Interest ratio is greater than the industry average, indicating they have a greater capacity to cover interest payments than industry peers.

As a quick aside, in the context of solvency ratios, "debt" doesn't refer to just debt with interest attached to it, but to total liabilities.

Basic Financial Accounting - Valuation Metrics

The first valuation metric investors typically become familiar with is the Price/Earnings ratio ("PE"). Public companies know this, which is why so much emphasis is placed on earnings figures, earnings-per-share ("EPS"), and "adjusted" EPS, even though these metrics don't always serve as the best barometers for true business value. Nonetheless, valuation metrics are an extremely useful tool to analyze how the sentiment around a company has changed over time. Let's take Shopify's 5-Year Price-to-Sales ratio as an example.

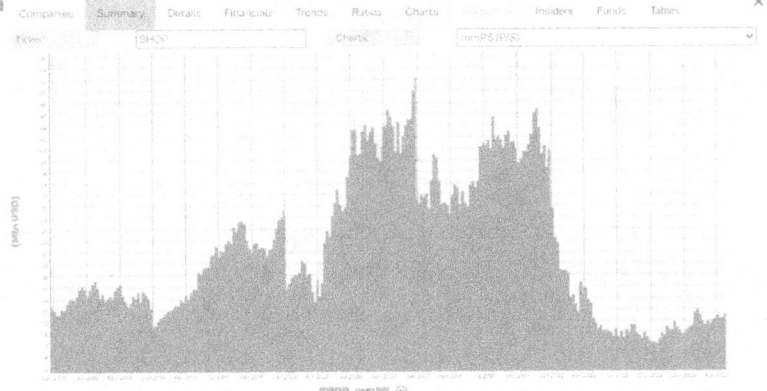

A higher P/S ratio means investors are more optimistic about a company's future and are valuing each dollar in sales that they generate rather highly. We can see that between July 2020 and October 2021 investors were very optimistic about Shopify's future, but then in early 2022 something happened which caused them to shift their sentiment. Again, it is important to analyze P/S ratios between companies that are in the same industry. Shopify's P/S will look very different from Exxon Mobil's.

For reference, below is Shopify's P/E ratio. We can see that it has fluctuated a lot more than the P/S because their earnings have been inconsistent over the past 5 years.

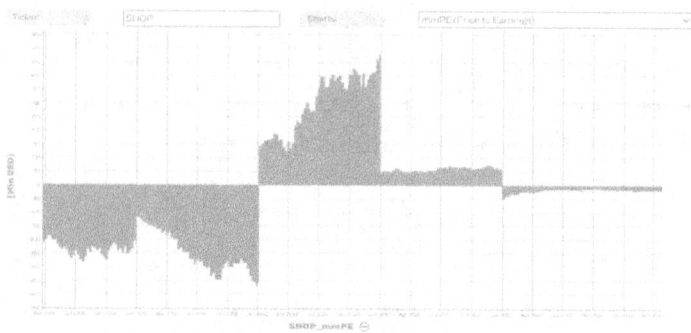

Another very important valuation metric is EV/EBITDA (Enterprise Value/EBITDA). This metric is used by investment bankers to understand how expensive/cheap companies within a given industry are being valued when they are acquired, taken public, or bought out. Enterprise value can be thought of as the cost to acquire a company debt-free. It is calculated as follows:

EV = Market capitalization + Total Debt + Total Preferred Stock Value + Minority Interests - Cash and Cash Equivalents

You may be familiar with all elements of the above calculation except for "Minority Interests". Due to accounting rules regarding consolidation, if a company owns majority interest in another company (i.e., they own more than 50% of the shares), they are required to "consolidate" that company in their financial statements. This means that all revenues, expenses, assets, liabilities, and equity pertaining to that company are included in the parent company's financials. So if the parent company only owns 75% of the shares of another company, then 25% of their financial results belong to "minority interests". So if we were to take over the entire company, we would also need to buy out the minority interests which is why they are included in the EV calculation.

Here is Shopify's 5-Year EV/EBITDA chart. We can see it has also fluctuated quite a bit:

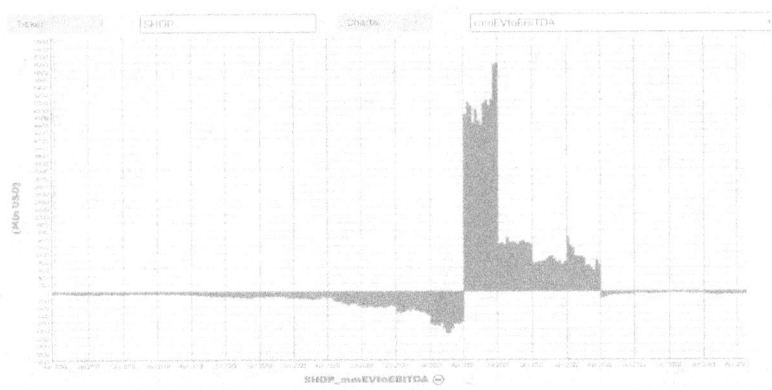

Risk, Reward and the CAPM

Now that we understand how to read and analyze basic financial information, let's discuss a topic that is more theoretical in nature, which is the relationship between risk and reward. There are very few fundamental laws of finance and investing, but one that is rarely ever disputed is the positive relationship between risk and return. If you want a higher potential return, then you have to be willing to take on more risk. In a way, investing is the process of deciding how much, and what type, of risks you are willing to accept depending on your goals, and then building a portfolio to match that. The riskiness of assets can range from US treasury bonds (least risky), to something like a small-cap biotech stock (extremely risky), and everything in between. US treasuries typically offer an annual return in the range of 0.5-5% (in recent decades) depending on what the central bank has set benchmark interest rates to. This rate is also referred to as the "risk-free rate" since there is very little doubt that the US government will fail to meet their debt obligations due to their economic scale and position as the world's reserve currency.

Below is a chart showing the 10-Year US Treasury Yield-to-Maturity has been over the past 10+ years:

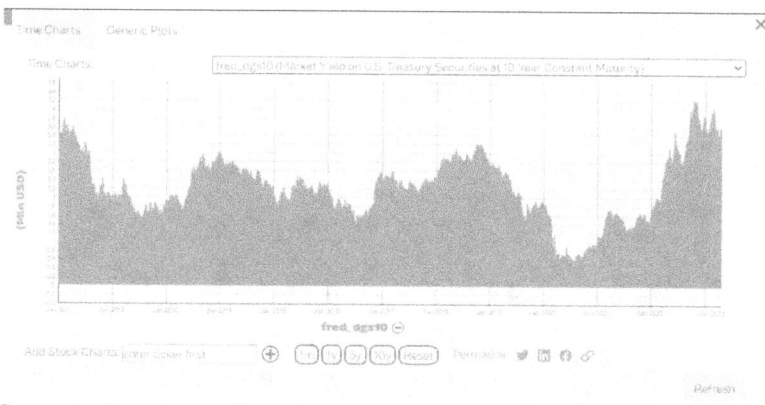

What the term "risk" actually refers to in investing is something that is still being figured out. Risk in its most simple form is the possibility that an investment's performance will differ from the expected performance, thus resulting in a possibility of loss. The two main types of risk that investors assume are systematic and unsystematic risk. Simply put, systematic risk is also referred to as market risk and is the risk that all investors in a given market are exposed to. This is a broad category, but it can include things like geopolitical risk, macroeconomic risk, currency risk, interest rate risk, and more.

Unsystematic risk refers to the risk you assume when you invest in a specific company or a specific industry. That company or industry could be exposed to particular risks that the broader market is not exposed to, such as a technological disruption, a change in management personnel, enactment of a new regulation, and more.

This is a theoretical definition of risk, but how can we quantitatively measure what risk is for a given asset? Whether it is a stock, bond, ETF, mutual fund, derivative, etc. We will discuss this more later in this book, but for now, let's discuss a simple metric to calculate a given stock's risk: beta. Beta measures how a stock's returns correlate in relation to a market index. A beta of 1 indicates that for every 1% a market index increases, the stock will increase by 1%, meaning the stock is not much more risky than the overall market (although it would still have its own set of unsystematic risks). A beta of 2 indicates a stock would move up by 2% for each 1% the market index moves up, and also it would move down 2% for each 1% the index moves down, thus its variation of returns are much greater making it more risky. It is important to note that beta is calculated based on historical return data and subject to change over time, and it will not precisely follow the pattern described above.

Below is an example of how Beta for Apple stock has changed over the past 5 years:

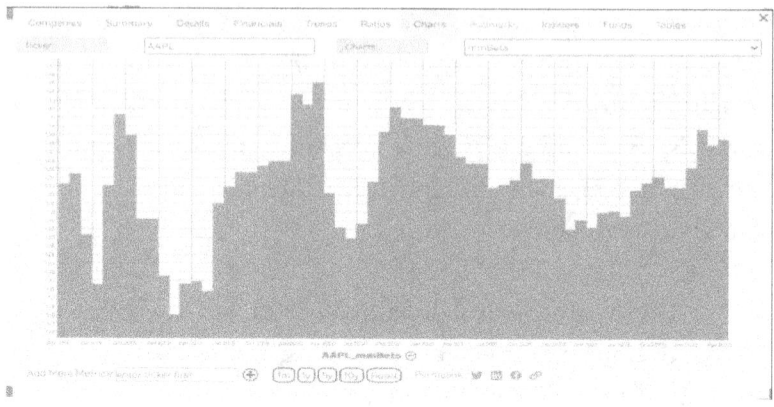

The CAPM is a practical application of the risk-reward relationship that makes use of beta. It stands for Capital Asset Pricing Model and it is used as a way to price common stocks. In this context, the term "price" is referring to calculating the *expected return* for a given stock. Because we cannot know what realized returns will be for a security prior to investing in them, expected returns are our proxy for what we expect returns will be given current data. The formula for the CAPM is as follows:

Expected Return = Risk Free Rate + Beta*Market Risk Premium

The *market risk premium* can be thought of as the additional expected return an investor receives by exposing themselves to the systematic risk of the market. It can be thought of as the expected return on the market (e.g., the S&P 500) minus the risk free rate. This market risk premium is usually somewhere in the 6-9% range, but can vary depending on market conditions, and it is also subject to debate.

We can see that this formula utilizes beta by ensuring that stocks with higher betas (i.e., more risky stocks) are assigned an expected return since beta is multiplied by the market risk premium.

The way you would use this formula in real investing is as the *cost of equity* for a company. Recall from before that companies can finance their operations either through the use of equity (selling common shares, preferred stock, or using cash flow from operations) or through debt. These two methods of funding operations are unique and have different costs and benefits associated with them. The cost of equity can be calculated using the CAPM, and the cost of debt can be found by determining the current yield-to-maturity on a company's debt. When we combine these, we get the *weighted average cost of capital* (*"WACC"*). Here is the formula:

WACC = Cost of Equity*(Value of Equity/(Value of Equity+Value of Debt)) + Cost of Debt*(Value of Debt/(Value of Equity+Value of Debt))

We can then use our calculated WACC as the discount rate for discounted the future cash flows earned by a business. Because this discount rate takes into account the riskiness of the asset by assigning a higher discount rate to more risky companies, it ensures we as investors are adequately compensating ourselves for the risk we take on when we invest. Cash flows earned by a small-cap biotech stock are much riskier than cash flows earned by a railroad company that has been in business for 150 years. And because money received today is worth more than money received in the future, and investors expect to be fairly compensated for taking on risk when investing, a company's future cash flows must be discounted at a discount rate.

Thinking about this practically may help you to understand it better. Let's say there is a company that is entirely funded by $100M worth of debt. The debt has an interest rate of 5% attached to it and the interest rate also happens to be the yield-to-maturity (YTM), and the company has a tax rate of 25%. Because this company has no equity, their cost of debt and WACC is 5%*(1-25%) = 3.75%. Due to the fact that interest payments are tax deductible, the cost of debt is lowered by the tax rate because the company saves on tax by paying interest which lowers their taxable income.

Let's now say the company then decides to raise $100M in equity through selling common stock. The risk free rate is 3%, the market risk premium is 8%, and the company's beta is 0.8. WACC would be calculated as follows:

WACC = 5%*(100/200)+(3%+0.8*8%)*(100/200)

WACC = 7.2%

Capital Allocation

Let's now tie this knowledge of risk, reward, and the cost of capital into the concept of capital allocation. You have probably heard the term "capital allocation" before. It is what public companies are constantly doing, they have limited capital in which to work with, and they have to make decisions on how to best allocate it. "Capital" can mean many different things in finance depending on the context, in this context we just mean funds that the business has acquired due to raising funding (debt or equity), or through their own operations. Understanding the concept of capital allocation is critical to understanding investing because companies that have demonstrated competence in this area tend to produce the best returns.

Below are some examples of how capital can be allocated:

- Mergers and acquisitions
- Paying down debt
- Paying dividends
- Buying back shares
- Reinvesting in the business (expanding production, research and development, hiring more employees, investing in a marketing campaign, etc.)

Every capital allocation decision has an expected payoff associated with it, and managers of businesses are trying to determine what those payoffs will be and how they can maximize them. The payoff of a capital allocation decision should exceed the cost of capital (WACC) in order for it to increase the value of the business

I think it is best to explain the concept of capital allocation using an example. Let's use our hypothetical company from the previous section that has a WACC of 7.2% and $200M in total funds raised evenly from debt and equity. Management has 3 options in which they can allocate capital:

Option 1: Invest the whole $200M in an apartment building that they can earn rental income from. They expect to earn $20M in after-tax rental income each year for the foreseeable future.

Option 2: Acquire another business for $200M that is currently generating $10M in earnings. Management also feels that they can use their expertise in cost-cutting to increase earnings to $12M/year. The business they want to acquire has no outstanding debt.

Option 3: Pay dividends to common shareholders.

Obviously, management's best option is Option #1. It produces the most after-tax cash flow, and it's the only option that increases the company's value. $20M in after-tax cash flow on a $200M investment is a 10% return, the company has a 7.2% cost of capital, so because their projected return on capital exceeds the cost to acquire capital, it is a good decision. That $20M can be returned to shareholders each year in the form of dividends, and then the apartment building can be sold in the future for $200M or possibly higher if real estate prices increase. This is clearly better than option 3 which involves just paying a dividend. Option 2 produces a 6% return ($12M/$200M), which is below cost of capital.

Option #2 also highlights the risk in valuing companies using basic financial metrics like P/E ratios. Even though earnings have increased from $10-12M/year, it doesn't mean the business is becoming more valuable because the expected return does not exceed WACC. But if you simply apply a constant P/E ratio to a company's earnings then you will think that it has.

If a company cannot identify any avenues to deploy their capital at a rate which is higher than their cost of capital, then their best option is to return cash to shareholders via dividends. Capital allocation is a much more complex area of finance and this section was designed to give you a quick primer on how to approach thinking about management decision-making and capital allocation decisions.

4
INVESTING IS JUST MATH

You could read a thousand books about investing and do ten years of practical buying and selling of investments, but without powerful tools at hand, it is almost impossible to beat S&P500... Indeed, the main objective of an individual investor is to beat those indices. Otherwise, one could just invest in the indices and go back to her day-to-day tasks forgetting about the whole investing matter. This book is about building up skills and learning the art of investing.

I call investing an art for a reason. There isn't one clearly defined mathematical way to beat the indices. So investing is "a complex probabilistic game where you have a lot of other players constantly affecting your own personal strategy". If this definition sounds confusing then please keep reading. By "complex probabilistic game" I define investing as a kind of a game where you play against other investors, because everyone wants to make a profit and this game is kind of "zero sum", meaning if one investor gains then someone else has to lose. By "a lot of other players constantly affecting your own personal strategy" I mean that the player's positions in such a "game" changes constantly and each player has to adapt quickly. So you need to develop the skill. You should become an artist. And like in any art a skillfully built portfolio is a work of **beauty**.

In most sciences things are precise and determined. For example, in a chess game you have the best defined strategy to win. The reason for the absence of such a perfect strategy in investing is very simple and it is explained in mathematical theory pretty well. The branch of math called - Game Theory deals with all kinds of "games". It is actually a pretty complex subject and has very little in common with what we, mere mortals, associate with computer "games" such as Call of Duty. So the Game Theory has a famous *Prisoner's Dilemma* game illustrating pretty well that even a very simple problem involving just two "players" can get complex very quickly:

> Two members of a criminal gang, A and B, are arrested and imprisoned. Each prisoner is in solitary confinement with no means of communication with their partner. The principal charge would lead to a sentence of ten years in prison; however, the police do not have the evidence for a conviction. They plan to sentence both to two years in prison on a lesser charge, but offer each prisoner a Faustian bargain: If one of them confesses to the crime of the principal charge, betraying the other, they will be pardoned and free to leave while the other must serve the entirety of the sentence instead of just two years for the lesser charge.

Moreover, Game Theory assumes that all "players" are perfectly rational, which as we know is far from reality. The players are defined as any rational actors that can make their own moves that affect the state of the game. In investing those would be individual investors, mutual fund managers, corporate CEOs, policymakers, and honestly every human on the planet (probably with a lesser degree of influence on the state of the stock market, but there are a lot of humans ;). Finally, Game Theory introduces probabilities in the mix and then tries to advise on how to get as close as possible to the unachievable **best winning strategy.**

Scientists tried to apply Game Theory to economics right from the beginning. In fact, the well-known Hollywood movie *Beautiful Mind* tells the story of John Forbes Nash, who was one of the early Game Theory mathematicians, and the one who was applying the theory in attempts to solve various economic problems. There are many Ph.D. papers written over the decades ever since Game Theory and Mathematical Economics exist. Those papers searched for ways of finding the optimal strategies and nothing really solved the problem of the perfect strategy. The theory explains why it is not possible very well.

The Game Theory explains it in terms of original players reacting rationally to the other player's rational actions, which in turn makes the original players change their strategies and vice versa. This creates a vicious cycle of "if he does this then I do that but if he knows I do this then he might do something else on which I react with that" and on and on. So if Warren Buffet bought Stock A today, it doesn't mean that in a few seconds after he did that you should be OK buying that same stock, because the "state" of the game has changed and the price, positions of the "players" and general market conditions have changed. Moreover, predicting what Warren Buffet will do also makes little sense because he is a smart fellow and he might think that a lot of investors like you are trying to predict his next move or react to his executed transactions and think and therefore change the state of the "game" so he might do something else instead. It is a similar situation to *Prisoner's Dilemma* as in that problem one prisoner thinks what the other prisoner would do and even thinks what the other prisoner thinks what the first prisoner would do and so on recursively.

So you might ask, what is the point then? Since nothing works and it is impossible to predict what other rational and irrational investors will do, or already did, how can one answer the ultimate question of investing: **Does the current stock price account for all available information and perfectly reflect the fair price? Game theory says - Yes! The fair price exists and theoretically can be found and it is part of - Game Theory Equilibrium.** I firmly believe that it is possible to get as close as possible to equilibrium, but it is just the opinion of the authors of this book.

What if we built a perfect simulation machine? Imagine if we had access to all market players' accounts, and to all the corporate reports, and all the policymakers' plans. We could build a perfect mathematical simulation of the market. We could make the best calculated investment decision assuming the most likely following reaction of other investors and then wait for the other "players" to make their decisions. Once those other players made their decisions and made their investments, which would inadvertently change the prices of stocks, we could repeat our cycle in our perfect simulation machine and make our next investment move. This would not allow for the best investing strategy because we cannot ever predict other investors' exact moves, especially since we cannot even assume, like in Game Theory, that they are absolutely rational players; but this simulation would give us the **best probabilistic strategy!**

We live in the real world and we cannot build a perfect simulation machine, nor can we get access to all the accounts of the players, or learn about the policymakers' future plans. We can only assume, estimate and predict. So we could only build the **best probabilistic strategy to the best of our knowledge.**

Now, this all sounds promising but how can we build the **best probabilistic strategy to the best of our knowledge?** The amount of information and the number of players one needs to simulate is beyond anything people have tried to simulate so far. I will not dive into the complexities of a simulation and all the details, but I will only give you a slight taste of what it takes to simulate an entire economy with all the companies, investors, policymakers, and all the relationships among them. Math has a tool to do just that. We call it in math – a graph. It looks like that:

Those circles are nodes and those lines are edges. The one thing to note about a graph is that the number of edges is usually much larger than the number of nodes. In the example above you can see only 7 nodes but 13 edges. As the number of nodes in a graph grows the number of edges usually grows much faster. Each node would correspond to a player when the economy simulated. The number of companies, individual investors, and policymakers is in the hundreds of thousands or possibly millions. The number of edges in such a graph will be billions or trillions because each node has so many relations with other nodes. Now to simulate the dynamics in such a complex system and to be able to predict the financial flows along the edges of the graph and ultimately supply/demand and thus the

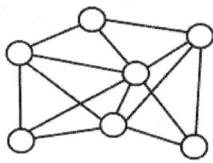

stock price, we would need to have specific numbers assigned to those nodes and edges. Only then would we be able to simulate such a complex system with some degree of fidelity. Give this task to an economics professor and he will start laughing nervously, because that is just an impossible task in today's world.

An animal tries to live and multiply. The world is incredibly complex and an animal is not very smart and doesn't fully understand the world around it. Yet an animal is perfectly capable of surviving in the world and sometimes even thriving. How can an animal do that? Instincts help a bit. Also, an animal learns a lot of right moves during childhood from its parents, which learned the right moves from their parents. The animal kingdom opened to mathematicians a whole class of new tools and algorithms – genetic algorithms, neural networks, artificial intelligence, etc. These tools allowed us to achieve **not-perfect** but **good enough** strategies in very complex systems. To achieve good investing results we do not need to simulate the whole economy. We need to develop certain heuristics, assumptions, and approximations that will give us a **good enough** investing strategy.

We are in the 21st century now and we are moving quickly beyond classics that had a few formulas tossed around to try to get us some good investing estimates. The discounted cash flow model to value a stock, even though nice and logical, is just too simple and naive for modern computing systems. In the next chapters of the book, we will explore algorithmic approaches to investing and building up our system step by step from the very simple programs a child can understand, to much more sophisticated techniques, yet explained plainly so that anyone can understand.

Let's begin!

5
HELLO WORLD

As I explained in the previous chapter it is not possible to be a good investor in the modern age without powerful tools. It is like asking a man with an abacus to calculate your taxes in the year 2023. It will take forever and by the time your taxes are done the next year arrives. Computers have to be used for effective investing!

Tickernomics is the investing research platform anyone can use for free. This platform allows you to write scripts, which can parse vast amounts of financial information and help you obtain unique insights into the market. The platform has a lot of scripts written by other people that happily share those scripts with everyone. We will not go that route in this book though. We will teach the reader to write her own scripts! It is a sweet feeling of being empowered to get **any** piece of information you need and to build and test **any** investing strategy that you want.

In order to get to that ultimate goal of beating the market we need to start slow and start with the simplest things. I will assume that you have never written a single line of code in your life. The scripting engine on the platform uses the scripting language Lua which Roblox popularized. Roblox is a gaming platform for kids specifically designed so children can do basic coding easily. If kids can do that then you, dear reader, can do that too. Also, you should not be concerned that something hard and complex is awaiting in the next chapters. If you did high school math at least at B level then it should all be easy!

We will start with the classic coding tutorial task of printing "Hello World" on a screen. Open Tickernomics at https://www.tickernomics.com and once you are in the system go to the My Scripts menu. Click New and you will see an almost empty coding screen:

```
My Scripts      Code      Log

1  function run()
2  end
```

All the coding happens between "function run()" and "end". Treat those two as markers of the beginning of the program and its end. So what code do we put in between those two markers to actually print "Hello World"? In order to know what commands are available for your use press Ctrl+Space. You will get the list of commands available in the system. Type "Print" and do code like the following and then click Run:

```
function run()
    Println("Hello World")
end
```

Once the system finishes processing, you will see the output similar to this:

```
initializing...
2023-01-24 04:08:12: Compiler:
2023-01-24 04:08:12: Queued.
2023-01-24 04:08:12: Run Script: New202312435231
2023-00-24 04:08:12: 140072007542528: Compiling Model Scripts
2023-00-24 04:08:12: 140072007542528: Done Compiling
2023-00-24 04:08:12: 140072007542528: Script run 2952, for user 5
2023-00-24 04:08:12: 140072007542528:
2023-01-24 04:08:12: Script output:
2023-01-24 04:08:12: Hello World
2023-00-24 04:08:12: 140072007542528:
2023-01-24 04:08:12: System Response:
2023-01-24 04:08:12: Finished Running.
```

You can see the "Hello World" output closer to the end of it (4th line from the bottom). The information before and after that text can sometimes be useful for debugging issues and measuring execution times.

Congratulations! You just did your first script. Of course, in no way it is impressive or useful, but it is a very important step in the understanding of how to do scripting to do investing research.

The next important step is to understand the variables. If you studied math, and I really hope that you did, then you did use variables in math. Those are usually Greek alphabet letters such as Δ or Ω, and sometimes English letters such as A, B, X, and Y. Scripts use variables a lot. They don't have to be numbered like in math, but can also be text variables. So, let's change our first script to use variables. The variables in Lua are declared with the special word – local. Let's declare a variable T(for Text) with the value "Hello World!":

```
function run()
   local T="Hello World!"
   PrintLn(T)
end
```

If we run this program we will get "Hello World!" printed and not "T", because T is a variable with the value "Hello World!" assigned earlier.

This program is still not impressive or useful. Stay patient as we are getting very close to demonstrating the main advantage of scripting. The difference is made by loops. Loops are what allow us to browse through millions of pieces of information automatically and find what we need. Let's add a loop to our little program.

First, let's assign a numeric value of 0 to our variable T and then use a new command "while" to start a loop. Then we add a condition that controls how long the loop runs. In our case, as we run this loop we will increase the value of variable T with each iteration. So let's run the loop ten times so our condition should be T < 10. Then we add the keyword "do" after which the loop code begins. The actual loop code will have variable T increment: T= T+1. The code that prints the value of T: PrintLn(T). Like everything in Lua, the loop ends with the "end" command. Here is the whole resulting code:

```
function run()
  local T=0
  while T < 10 do
    T=T+1
    PrintLn(T)
  end
end
```

Here is the output:

```
2023-01-24 05:07:59: 1
2023-01-24 05:07:59: 2
2023-01-24 05:07:59: 3
2023-01-24 05:07:59: 4
2023-01-24 05:07:59: 5
2023-01-24 05:07:59: 6
2023-01-24 05:07:59: 7
2023-01-24 05:07:59: 8
2023-01-24 05:07:59: 9
2023-01-24 05:07:59: 10
```

You could easily print this by writing the print command ten times, but what if we needed to print the names of all NASDAQ-listed companies? Would you write it manually for each company or would you rather use a loop to print thousands of companies? I think by now you should be getting where I am going with this. Let's print all the companies available in the system!

In order to print all companies we need to learn two of the functions to call. We learn about all the functions available in the system using the Help file that can be opened by going to the Info menu and then to the Help menu. The two functions we are interested in are:

GetTickerCount() retrieve the number of companies

GetTickerByIndex() retrieve the ticker of the company by company index

As you can see from the Help file, GetTickerCount will give you the number of companies in the system, so we can edit our existing loop code and replace "T < 10" with "T < GetTickerCount()". The second function simply returns the ticker by the index specified. An index is just a number in the range from the first company denoted by the number zero to the last company denoted by the max number of companies minus one. So we can call GetTickerByIndex(T) to get the ticker value using the index number T. Here is the resulting code:

```
function run()
  local T=0
  while T < GetTickerCount() do
    local ticker=GetTickerByIndex(T)
    T=T+1
    PrintLn(ticker)
  end
end
```

As you can see we had to introduce a new variable that we called "ticker". We could have called it B or anything else but naming variables more descriptively helps to make your code more readable. As this while loop runs, the variable T will change from 0 to 1 and then to 2 and so on until reaching the max number of companies. Calling GetTickerByIndex(0) will give the first ticker of the first company, then calling GetTickerByIndex(1) will give us the ticker of the second company and so on. If you run this code you will see a huge list of all the company tickers available in the system. If at this moment you do not understand how this works please read this chapter again, because this is the most important part of all the coding explained in this book, and you really need to understand how this loop produced the output that you see.

Not everyone knows about companies by their ticker symbols, so why don't we modify our script and print company names as well so those people who forgot what ticker MMM stands for can see the company name too. The Help file tells us that we can use this nice command:

GetCompanyPropStr(ticker, string propName) retrieve company string property. Supported properties: Name, Exchange, Industry,WebSite,Description, CEO,Sector, Tags,Address, State,City, Zip, Country, Phone. Industry and Sector lists are avaialble.

This command retrieves a string (i.e., a line of text) property for a given company. This can be the company name, industry, sector, address, etc. One of the supported properties is Name. So let's modify our script and call this command to get the company name. We will also use the ".." operator which concatenates (i.e., connects) text together. Here is what we should get:

```
function run()
  local T=0
  while T < GetTickerCount() do
    local ticker=GetTickerByIndex(T)
    local compName=GetCompanyPropStr(ticker,"Name")
    T=T+1
    PrintLn(ticker .. "  " .. compName)
  end
end
```

The result output:

```
2023-01-25 01:27:20: Script output:
2023-01-25 01:27:20: AAPL  Apple Inc.
2023-01-25 01:27:20: MSFT  MICROSOFT CORP
2023-01-25 01:27:20: GOOGL  Alphabet Inc.
2023-01-25 01:27:20: TSLA  Tesla Inc.
2023-01-25 01:27:20: BRK-B  BERKSHIRE HATHAWAY INC
2023-01-25 01:27:20: UNH  UNITEDHEALTH GROUP INC
2023-01-25 01:27:20: JNJ  JOHNSON & JOHNSON
```

6
FIRST FINANCIAL RESULTS

In this chapter we will mine financial data for the first time. Let's start by finding the stocks with the highest revenue growth. We will write a script that obtains the companies' revenue. We will then calculate the growth percentage of the revenue and only print out companies that had revenue growth of 50% or more. Then you can research each company individually to find out reasons why revenue grew so much and maybe you will identify a company to invest in from the list.

In order to find such companies we will need to learn a new very powerful command:

GetXBRL(string ticker, int day, string segment, string valueName)

This first "string ticker" argument for the GetXBRL command identifies the company of interest. The second argument specifies the day for which you want to get the value. The "segment" argument should just be an empty string as it is reserved for the future when segment data becomes available. Finally, the valueName argument identifies the value you want to know. In our case, we want to know the revenue for the last 12 months. So valueName should be "mmRevenueTTM", where TTM stands for Twelve Trailing Months and mm stands for Main Metric. All possible other valueNames can be found in the Help page's section on the GetXBRL function.

The "day" argument needs some explanation. The Tickernomics system deals with time as a progression of days from day one. Day one is when Tickernomics started collecting data, which was around the year 2011. The system's total number of days in year 2025 is roughly 14 years * 365 days=5110. So today's day has an index around that number. This is perfect for writing algorithms as it is very easy to use addition and subtraction of days to get to the exact date/time period you need. For example, if today's day index is 5110 then a day one week ago would be 5110-7=5103. Two very helpful functions are provided to deal with day indices:

GetTotalDays() retrieve the total number of accessible days in the system
GetTodayDay() gets the index of the today's day in the system

For example, to get the revenue for MSFT (Microsoft) one month ago from today would look like this:

```
GetXBRL("MSFT",GetTodayDay()-30,"","mmRevenueTTM")
```

We are ready now to modify the script from the previous chapter to print revenues for all companies:

```
function run()
  local T=0
  while T < GetTickerCount() do
    local ticker=GetTickerByIndex(T)
    local today=GetTodayDay()
    local compRevenue=GetXBRL(ticker,today,"","mmRevenueTTM")
    T=T+1
    PrintLn(ticker .. "  " .. compRevenue)
  end
end
```

Some revenues might be zero in the script output and that is either because the ticker,such as SPY, is just an index fund or the system doesn't have revenue information:

```
2023-01-25 03:44:27: PG  81253.049180328
2023-01-25 03:44:27: SPY  0.0
2023-01-25 03:44:27: JPM  123431.0
2023-01-25 03:44:27: WMT  573884.875
```

Let's modify the script so it also retrieves revenue 12 months ago and it calculates revenue growth by subtracting

today's revenue from the prior year's revenue and dividing by
the prior year's revenue:

```
function run()
  local T=0
  while T < GetTickerCount() do
    local ticker=GetTickerByIndex(T)
    local today=GetTodayDay()
    local pastDay=today - 12*30
    local compRevenue=GetXBRL(ticker,today,"","mmRevenueTTM")
    local compRevenuePast=GetXBRL(ticker,pastDay,"","mmRevenueTTM")
    local percent = 100*(compRevenue - compRevenuePast)/compRevenuePast
    T=T+1
    PrintLn(ticker .. "  " .. compRevenue .."  "..
        compRevenuePast .. " " .. percent)
  end
end
```

The result might have some of the values as "nan". That
translates as Not A Number and it is a result of division by zero
for companies that do not have revenue in the system. Another
thing you would notice is that the list is so huge and so cluttered
that it is not very useful, so it is time to filter it for those high-
revenue growth companies.

In order to filter the companies in our code, we need to
use the most fundamental if-then statement. If-then statements
check if a condition is true or false, and if it is true it will execute
the code located after the "then" part of the if-then statement.
We want to only print the companies that have revenue growth
above 50% so let's add the following code:

```
if percent > 50 and compRevenuePast>0 then
    PrintLn(ticker .. "   " .. compRevenue .."  "..
        compRevenuePast .. " " .. percent)
end
```

The code between "if" and "then" checks for two
conditions:

- Does growth percent above 50%?
- Is past revenue above zero?

The code between "then" and "end" will only execute if **both** conditions are true. So it will only print the company if those conditions are met. We could add as many conditions to the if-then statement as we like by using "and" to indicate that both conditions must be met for the if-then statement to be true. If you run the code you will see only the companies you are interested in:

```
2023-01-26 00:27:43: Script output:
2023-01-26 00:27:43: TM  9406136.7598401  240710.22383168 3807.6598451496
2023-01-26 00:27:43: COP  79397.5  49359.955882353 60.854074078267
2023-01-26 00:27:43: INFY  13707.678113748  2044231081283 6605.5423622389
2023-01-26 00:27:43: AMOV  249260.20006938  47892.620179102 420.4563858424
2023-01-26 00:27:43: LCID  161.95217364253  58.318904411765 177.70098782902
2023-01-26 00:27:43: SQM  8661.27  4471.4373013699 93.702145780878
2023-01-26 00:27:43: IBKR  3841.5  2481.75 54.789966757329
2023-01-26 00:27:43: RIVN  1224.5  109.92978345184 1013.8928519189
```

The final improvement to our script in this chapter will be the decrease of its size by one line. The line we will get rid of is:

```
T=T+1
```

Somehow the perfectionists in the coding world thought that it is too vulgar to have a line like this in loops, so they invented a different syntax for loops. Those other kinds of loops are called for-loops. We will replace two lines: T=T+1 line and our "while" line with one line like this:

```
for T=0,GetTickerCount(),1 do
```

The for loop combines those two lines into one line. It also runs code between "do" and "end" a certain number of times. It automatically increments the variable T by 1 until

GetTickerCount() number is reached. So the for-loop has three components specified which are separated by commas: the initial value (T=0); the max number (GetTickerCount()); and the increment: 1.

Here is the final code for this chapter:

```
function run()
    local T=0
    for T=0,GetTickerCount(),1 do
        local ticker=GetTickerByIndex(T)
        local today=GetTodayDay()
        local pastDay=today - 12*30
        local compRevenue=GetXBRL(ticker,today,"","mmRevenueTTM")
        local compRevenuePast=GetXBRL(ticker,pastDay,"","mmRevenueTTM")
        local percent = 100*(compRevenue - compRevenuePast)/compRevenuePast
        if percent > 50 and compRevenuePast>0 then
            PrintLn(ticker .. "  " .. compRevenue .." "..
                compRevenuePast .. " " .. percent)
        end
    end
end
```

7
LOOKING FOR STABLE DIVIDENDS

Humans like to categorize things. Scientists put every new animal that they discover into some kind of classification. In reality nature is "analog" and not "digital" and sometimes it is very hard to choose the right category for the transient kinds of animals or plants. Is a tomato a berry, fruit, or vegetable? Science clearly defines its category but in practice it is hard to classify especially for cherry tomatoes. The same happens with stocks. You often hear one stock called "a growth stock" and another being called "a value stock", yet other stocks can be called "a dividend stock". I personally don't like those classifications. To me, all stocks are just stocks that have certain parameters. The beauty of scripting in stock picking is that scripts just browse through **all** of the stocks.

Today we will write a new script to search for stocks that can form the foundation for a dividend income portfolio. We will not search just for stocks paying high dividends though. Instead, we will analyze 5 parameters of the stocks and try to find the ideal good balance of those parameters to ensure we pick dividend stocks that provide us with a reliable source of income in the long run.. We will also utilize some filtering to give certain stocks a better chance to show up on top of the results.

The following dividend stock-picking strategy is only one of many possible strategies. The goal of this exercise is not to just teach you on specific dividend investing strategy, but to show you what is possible with scripting so you can use it to formulate and research your own ideas. For this script, we will analyze the following five parameters of a stock:

□   dividend yield – dividend as % of a stock price

- capitalization – stock price multiplied by the number of shares outstanding
- debt to capitalization ratio – company debt divided by a capitalization
- revenue growth(TTM) – annual revenue today minus annual revenue 12 months ago divided by the same
- shares outstanding change(TTM) – number of stocks available for purchase and owned by investors

These 5 parameters need some explanation. The dividend yield is obvious and you want that as high as possible. Unfortunately, a lot of high dividend-paying companies are doing that out of desperation to keep their stock price afloat, because many other parameters of such companies are terrible. Often high dividend-paying companies have high debt, or their revenue steadily declines as the business dies out over the years, or the company issues too much new stock diluting existing investors. So you cannot just look at dividend yield when picking a good long-term dividend source. You want to continue receiving your dividends for a long period of time and you don't want many surprises along the way! That means the company should be "significant in the economy" and "stable". Let's look at the other 4 parameters.

The size of the company matters! Historically larger companies have lower volatility, they also collapse and go bust more rarely. So you, given all other parameters equal, would normally prefer a larger company as your dividend source. Hence you have the capitalization parameter.

The debt-to-capitalization ratio is a great parameter to measure how significant the debt size of a company is. You can't just use debt because a billion dollars of debt for Microsoft is nothing, but a billion dollars of debt for a $500M company could be detrimental. So you want to measure the debt relative to the company's size.

Revenue growth is one of the most important parameters for our dividend payers search because revenue stagnation is often the primary reason for high dividend yields to keep companies attractive for investors. So we want to account for that when balancing dividend yield and revenue growth.

Finally the shares outstanding change parameter will give us protection against companies that constantly issue new shares, diluting existing investors. I have noticed that this is a favorite trick of high dividend-paying REITs.

Let's use the previous chapter's script and modify it so we can pull those 5 parameters for each company (I marked the new additions):

```
function run()
   local T=0
   for T=0,GetTickerCount(),1 do
      local ticker=GetTickerByIndex(T)
      local today=GetTodayDay()
      local pastDay=today - 12*30
      local compRevenue=GetXBRL(ticker,today,"","mmRevenueTTM")
      local compRevenuePast=GetXBRL(ticker,pastDay,"","mmRevenueTTM")
      local divid=GetXBRL(ticker,today,"","mmDividendYield")
      local cap=GetXBRL(ticker,today,"","mmCapitalization")
      local debtToCap=GetXBRL(ticker,today,"","mmDebtToCapital")
      local stocksGrowth = GetXBRL(ticker,today,"","mmSharesOutstandingGrowthYoY")

      local percent = 100*(compRevenue - compRevenuePast)/compRevenuePast
      if percent >= 0 and compRevenuePast>0 then
         PrintLn(ticker .. " " .. percent .." ".. 
              divid .. " " .. cap .. " " .. debtToCap .. " " .. stocksGrowth)
      end
   end
end
```

Running this code will print all 5 parameters for each

company:

AAPL 0.3876900850107 0.78095307173424 2250840.66553 236.9533470161 -2.7167393597861
MSFT 4.0573971332136 1.082341187245 1798046.7 34.731456621689 -1.0836527025241

You are probably complaining at this point that the numbers printed are hard to read as they have too many digits in the fractional part. How about making it look like this:

AAPL 0.39 0.78 2250840.67 236.95 -2.72
MSFT 4.06 1.08 1798046.70 34.73 -1.08

Each number only has 2 digits in the fractional part. You can achieve this with Lua's string.format command:

```
Your Number Rounded=string.format("%.2f",Your Number)
```

.2f means two digits after dot, and "f" stands for floating point number.

Here is the modified portion of script that produces the nicer print out:

```
if percent >= 0 and compRevenuePast>0 then
    percent=string.format("%.2f",percent)
    divid=string.format("%.2f",divid)
    cap=string.format("%.2f";cap)
    debtToCap=string.format("%.2f",debtToCap)
    stocksGrowth=string.format("%.2f",stocksGrowth)

    PrintLn(ticker .. " " .. percent .." "..
        divid .. " " .. cap .. " " .. debtToCap .. " " .. stocksGrowth)
end
```

It is now time to build the ranking system based on all 5 very diverse parameters. The revenue percent change can vary from negative hundreds to positive hundreds for different companies. The dividend yield can be zero to up to 50s for some super high-risk companies. Capitalization can be from 10(this number is in millions) for tiny companies to 2000000 for trillion-dollar-valued giants such as Apple. The debt to Capitalization ratio varies widely and can be zero to thousands,so we can filter out anything above 300 to account for significant anomalies that will skew the results and use 300 for the rest as the maximum. Finally Outstanding Shares Growth percentage is usually less than -+5% but can jump a lot for some companies which we will cut off. So how can we bring all these parameters together?

Usually, mathematicians bring different parameters placed in the same formula to a common denominator, and in science the favorite standardized range for a compound parameter is [-1;+1]. So to bring each of the five components to the [-1;+1] range we need to divide each of them by their corresponding max value. If a parameter has any significant outliers then those can be filtered out by if-then checks. Here is the code to standardize all of the five parameters:

```
local percentRevenueSt=percent/100
local dividSt=divid/50
local capSt=cap/2000000
local debtToCapSt = debtToCap/300
local stocksGrowthSt = stocksGrowth/5
```

Now those five parameters should have a roughly [-1;+1] range. We are all set to build the rank formula. If we just add up all five parameters together we should get an equally weighted rank, but in math when people build the cost functions (more scientific name for rank) the weight coefficients are used to properly balance the importance of each of the components in a cost function formula, because in majority of cases the components are not equally important!

Here is the generic formula for our rank:

```
local rank = w1*percentRevenueSt + w2*dividSt + w3*capSt
                   - w4*debtToCapSt - w5*stocksGrowthSt
```

Did you notice that debtToCapSt and stocksGrowthSt have minus in front? We are looking for the best company to invest in for a stable dividend income. So if the company has high debt or if the company issues too many new shares then it makes that company less desirable for investment, and that is why those two components being higher will negatively impact the rank.

w1,w2,w3,w4,w5 are weights. Currently, if we made all of the weights just equal to one then the range of the rank would be [-3;+3]. To keep the range and weight management easier to control, the weights' total sum should normally be equal to 1. We should preserve the original ranges of the components when summing the components up. So w1+w2+w3+w4+w5=1. We should now decide on the exact values for our weights. That is when the true art of investing comes into play!

Math has a term for picking the right weights just by someone's intuition – heuristics. When a mathematician cannot figure out the precise method to find something, but he feels the method he prefers works somehow, then he would say "I employ heuristics here" just to sound more professional. Same with me. I will use specific weight numbers that worked well for me in the past, but of course, the picked weights might not be optimal and might not work in the future. At least you know what weights mean – they increase or decrease the relative importance of each of the five components. So feel free to play with your own weight picks. Here is my final formula:

```
local rank = 0.3*percentRevenueSt + 0.4*dividSt + 0.1*capSt
            - 0.1*debtToCapSt - 0.1*stocksGrowthSt
```

We will also add some if-then statements to filter out any outliers, and finally we will only print companies with a very high rank to avoid clutter. We should not necessarily take the highest ranking company as our best choice, because there are so many other factors besides those 5 for each company, so we need to print all the high ranking ones and then manually research them and pick the best.

Here are some of the picks I got:

```
MIXT  396.84  3.35 160.70 60.11 -1.76
BEDU  419.82  99.40 76.30 82.35 0.00
ETI-P  198.13  5.54 1127.77 213.96 -77.18
AKO-B  6.70  6.10 2158.25 122.80 -50.00
HCXY  6.66  6.33 3.19 112.08 -99.76
EAI  4.68  5.42 1059.40 132.87 -76.62
ENO  6.45  5.73 203.05 7.73 -95.80
```

A diligent investor should go through the suggested list manually and do an in-depth analysis to pick the true winner. It is much easier to do the analysis when you have a pre-selected list of 20-30 picks than to do it through thousands of stocks, and this is the true power of scripting. Here is the final code for this chapter:

8
AGGREGATING FINANCIAL DATA

It would be useful to know the industry sector trends. It is very important to evaluate companies in relation to other

```
function run()
  local T=0
  for T=0,GetTickerCount(),1 do
    local ticker=GetTickerByIndex(T)
    local today=GetTodayDay()
    local pastDay=today - 12*30
    local compRevenue=GetXBRL(ticker,today,"","mmRevenueTTM")
    local compRevenuePast=GetXBRL(ticker,pastDay,"","mmRevenueTTM")
    local divid=GetXBRL(ticker,today,"","mmDividendYield")
    local cap=GetXBRL(ticker,today,"","mmCapitalization")
    local debtToCap=GetXBRL(ticker,today,"","mmDebtToCapital")
    local stocksGrowth = GetXBRL(ticker,today,"","mmSharesOutstandingGrowthYoY")
    local percent = 100*(compRevenue - compRevenuePast)/compRevenuePast
    if  percent < 500 and percent >= 0 and compRevenuePast>0 and divid>0.5
      and debtToCap>=0  and debtToCap < 300 and cap>0 and stocksGrowth<5 then
        local percentRevenueSt=percent/100
        local dividSt=divid/50
        local capSt=cap/2000000
        local debtToCapSt = debtToCap/300
        local stocksGrowthSt = stocksGrowth/5
        local rank = 0.3*percentRevenueSt + 0.4*dividSt + 0.1*capSt
                       - 0.1*debtToCapSt - 0.1*stocksGrowthSt
      if rank > 1 then
          percent=string.format("%.2f",percent)
          divid=string.format("%.2f",divid)
          cap=string.format("%.2f",cap)
          debtToCap=string.format("%.2f",debtToCap)
          stocksGrowth=string.format("%.2f",stocksGrowth)
          PrintLn(ticker .. "  " .. percent .." ".. 
              divid .. " " .. cap .. "  " .. debtToCap .. " " .. stocksGrowth)
      end
    end
  end
end
```

companies within the same industry, and it is never a good idea to compare companies from different sectors without consideration of their corresponding industries. Comparing a bank's total assets and a mining company's total assets is almost meaningless because a big part of a bank's assets are loans issued to other entities while a mining company's assets are mostly leasing rights to mining sites and equipment. The Price to Sales ratio for Walmart is less than 1, while the Price to Sales for Relay Therapeutics, Inc. is above 1000. So the P/S ratio for those companies is incomparable because Walmart sells an unimaginable volume of products and makes money on a tiny fraction of those sales. On the other hand, Relay Therapeutics is a biotech research company making almost no sales and the valuation of that company is based on R&D and know-how. Understanding the importance of the economic sector in which the company operates is crucial to building proper algorithms for stock picking. We will learn how to aggregate data from economic sectors in this chapter.

We have to learn a new concept in scripting so we can easily aggregate data. It is called an array in Lua. It is a special type of variable that can contain a lot of data pieces. Moreover, you can easily extract the data pieces in the array using an index. I know it sounds confusing and complicated for those readers that are not familiar with coding, but I will explain arrays in a very simple way unrelated to coding, but using your favorite childhood toy – Legos.

Think of some Lego bricks in a pile. Wouldn't you like to have them ordered so you can pick the right brick quickly when the need comes? So let's order the bricks in a line. For now, we will just pick one brick at a time and put them in a nicely arranged line. We will learn how to sort the bricks by their kind later. So here is how it will look after we go through the whole pile:

Now each brick has a unique index by which we can identify it. The first brick has an index of one and the last brick has an index of 4. That is all you need to understand about arrays because an array is an ordered and indexed list of objects, nothing more. You declare an array like this in Lua:

```
local industries={}
```

"industries" is just the name of this new variable and {} indicates it is an array. You place "bricks" or items in the array like so:

```
local industries={}
industries[1]="Retail"
industries[2]="Banks"
```

"Retail" is placed at index of one and "Banks" is placed at index of two. Now, a single variable "industries" stores two items. Then you can print the contents of the array variable using the special for-loop:

```
local industries={}
industries[1]="Retail"
industries[2]="Banks"
for ind,value in ipairs(industries) do
    PrintLn(ind .. "  " .. value)
end
```

ipairs(industries) gives two things from the array: index and the value of that index, which is assigned to the for-loop temporary variables "ind" and "value". The PrintLn prints the index and the value for that index. This special for-loop will run through all of the items stored in the array. So here is the output from this little program:

```
Script output:
1 Retail
2 Banks
```

With this new knowledge of arrays, we are all set to aggregate large amounts of financial data. Let's try looking at revenue growth by industry. It would be financially diligent to

71

identify economic sectors where revenue growth was high last year. For example, if a company comes from an industry that saw high growth then seeing 20% growth within a specific company coming from that industry wouldn't be that impressive. On the contrary, seeing a 20% percent revenue growth of a company coming from an industry that saw a decline in revenue would mark that company as outstanding and interesting for closer inspection. A script like this could be useful for identifying companies that are significantly outperforming their industry, whether it's due to a unique competitive advantage, a new product/service they recently introduced, a new market they have expanded into, or another reason. We will declare the industries array variable and also write a for-loop to go through all companies as we did in the earlier chapters of the book:

```
function run()
    local industries={}
    for i=0,GetTickerCount(),1 do
        local ticker=GetTickerByIndex(i)
    end -- this is how you write comments
end
```

The next task is to get revenue for today and for a year ago and then calculate the percent change in the revenue. Then we need to add that revenue to the specific sector of the economy. We will use the function GetCompanyPropStr to get the company's sector name.

```
function run()
    local industries={}
    for i=0,GetTickerCount(),1 do
        local ticker=GetTickerByIndex(i)
        local sector = GetCompanyPropStr(ticker,"Sector")
    end -- this is how you write comments
end
```

The next step is to retrieve the revenue for today and for a year ago for each company and then record it in the industries array for each industry. There is a problem though. We want to get the average growth of revenue for each industry stored in the industries array once the for-loop finishes going through all of the companies. Do you know how to calculate averages? You sum up values and then divide by the number of those values. We have an array to store revenues for each industry - "industries", but we do not have an array to store the number of companies for each industry. We will need to store that so we can divide all the revenues that we collected by this number to get the average value. So we will add another array variable called "industryCompanyCount". Here is how we get revenues for today and the past as well as how we record revenue change and the number of companies in each industry:

```
local industries={}
local industryCompanyCount={}
local today=GetTodayDay()
local past=today-365
for i=0,GetTickerCount(),1 do
    local ticker=GetTickerByIndex(i)
    local sector = GetCompanyPropStr(ticker,"Sector")
    local revenueNow=GetXBRL(ticker,today,"","mmRevenueTTM")
    local revenuePast=GetXBRL(ticker,past,"","mmRevenueTTM")
    if revenuePast > 0 then
        local revenueChange=100*(revenueNow-revenuePast)/revenuePast
        local origValue=industries[sector] or 0
        industries[sector]=origValue+revenueChange
        origValue=industryCompanyCount[sector] or 0
        industryCompanyCount[sector]=origValue+1
    end
end -- end of the first loop where data is aggregated
```

The only tricky line to understand here is this one:

```
local origValue=industries[sector] or 0
```

We are trying to get the current value stored for the sector in the industries array. What if there are no values stored for the sector in the array? Nothing is stored in the array when we only begin to go through each company and the industries array is completely empty. In that case, the value will be "nil" for industries[sector] or in the English language we would call it "none". The code piece: "or 0" will convert "none" to zero.This is what we want to be stored in the origValue variable if there are no values yet for the specified sector. The next line is very easy to understand now:

```
industries[sector]=origValue+revenueChange
```

Here we add the newly calculated revenueChange value to the originally stored value in the industries array for the sector corresponding to the current company in the loop. So if the loop continues to run the industries[sector] will keep adding up revenue change values. In order to be able to calculate the average later we should also record the number of companies for each industry:

```
origValue=industryCompanyCount[sector] or 0
industryCompanyCount[sector]=origValue+1
```

Lets print the contents of both arrays by iterating through them with the new for-loop (notice that ipairs is replaced with pairs because our index is a sector name which is a string and not a number; i stands for integer number in the original ipairs):

```
for key,value in pairs(industries) do
    local companyNumber=industryCompanyCount[key]
    PrintLn(key .. "    " .. value .. "    " .. companyNumber)
end
```

"key" and "value" are key-value pairs returned for each entry in the "industries" array. Here is the output that we get that prints the sector name, the accumulated sum of revenue changes and the number of companies in the sector:

Utilities 2135.9226548417 151
Consumer Cyclical 9651.2597076471 610
Consumer Defensive 1056.1283408332 278

The only thing we need to do now is calculate the average by dividing the accumulated sum of revenue changes by the number of companies in the sector and also filter companies with crazy revenue changes so they don't skew our averages.

Here is the final code for this chapter:

As you can see we have the main for-loop that goes through each company. We retrieve ticker,sector, current revenue and past revenue for each company. Then we calculate revenue change, filter revenue changes below 300 and finally record the result for each company into two arrays: one for revenue changes and one for company counts. Then we have another pairs-loop that goes through the contents of the resulting arrays

```
local industries={}
local industryCompanyCount={}
local today=GetTodayDay()
local past=today-365
for i=0,GetTickerCount(),1 do
    local ticker=GetTickerByIndex(i)
    local sector = GetCompanyPropStr(ticker,"Sector")
    local revenueNow=GetXBRL(ticker,today,"","mmRevenueTTM")
    local revenuePast=GetXBRL(ticker,past,"","mmRevenueTTM")
    if revenuePast > 0 then
        local revenueChange=100*(revenueNow-revenuePast)/revenuePast
        if math.abs(revenueChange) < 300 then
            local origValue=industries[sector] or 0
            industries[sector]=origValue+revenueChange
            origValue=industryCompanyCount[sector] or 0
            industryCompanyCount[sector]=origValue+1
        end
    end
end -- end of the first loop where data is aggregated

for key,value in pairs(industries) do
    local companyNumber=industryCompanyCount[key]
    local avg=math.floor(value/companyNumber)
    PrintLn(key .. "    " .. avg)
end
```

and we print their content and the average.

9

OUTLIERS IN THEIR SECTORS

Since we have the array with average revenue changes for each sector, we can now go through the companies again and find the true revenue growth outliers within their respective industries. Let's reuse the code from Chapter 8 and add a for-loop to the end of the script to go through all companies again and calculate revenue change for each company. Only this time we will also extract average revenue change for the company's industry recorded in the arrays from the Chapter 8. If the average revenue change is less than 100%, then we would print this company and consider it an outlier within that industry. Here are the added lines of code:

```
                                   ⦿
                                   ⦿
                                   ⦿
end -- end of the first loop where data is aggregated

for key,value in pairs(industries) do
     local companyNumber=industryCompanyCount[key]
     local avg=math.floor(value/companyNumber)
     industries[key]=avg -- we store the average in industries array
end -- end second loop where we store averages

for i=0,GetTickerCount(),1 do
     local ticker=GetTickerByIndex(i)
     local sector = GetCompanyPropStr(ticker,"Sector")
     local revenueNow=GetXBRL(ticker,today,"","mmRevenueTTM")
     local revenuePast=GetXBRL(ticker,past,"","mmRevenueTTM")
     if revenuePast > 0 then
          local revenueChange=100*(revenueNow-revenuePast)/revenuePast
          if math.abs(revenueChange) < 300 then
            local industryAvg=industries[sector]
            local outlierPercent=revenueChange-industryAvg
            if outlierPercent>100 then
              PrintLn(sector .. "  " .. ticker ..  "  " ..
                    industryAvg .. "  " .. math.floor(revenueChange))
            end
          end
     end
end -- end of the third loop where we search outliers
```

And here are the "alpha-males" of their respective industries printed out(they exceeded their industry average revenue growth by at least 100%) :

```
2023-01-29 14:43:05: Script output:
2023-01-29 14:43:07: Consumer Cyclical LCID 5 177
2023-01-29 14:43:07: Consumer Cyclical CCL 5 265
2023-01-29 14:43:07: Consumer Cyclical CUK 5 195
2023-01-29 14:43:07: Consumer Cyclical RCL 5 105
2023-01-29 14:43:07: Healthcare AZTA 2 111
2023-01-29 14:43:07: Healthcare ASND 2 124
2023-01-29 14:43:07: Consumer Cyclical NCLH 5 258
2023-01-29 14:43:07: Energy CIVI 30 235
2023-01-29 14:43:07: Energy BSM 30 152
2023-01-29 14:43:07: Financial Services JXN -11 185
2023-01-29 14:43:07: Financial Services ONB -11 105
```

This is the power you get from scripting. Screw passive investing! Of course, this is still just a very simple report and you could build a much more sophisticated multi-factor rank of success for each respective industry. I will leave that to your creativity, because every person, every investor has the right to be an independent artist and build his own beautiful strategy.

Aren't you tired of these geeky printouts? How about generating the data and placing it in a reusable table that you can export to Excel? Let's learn that.

Tickernomics supports Tables. You can create a table in your script and it will show up in the Tickernomics UI under the Insight Tables menu. Then once it is visible in Tables, you can export it to excel. A table has some key properties: a name, the number of columns, the number of rows, column headers, and row headers. Therefore, the command to create a table has to have a lot of arguments: *CreateTable(<table name>,<column number>,<row number>,<comma separated list of column names>,<comma separated list of row names>,<table description>)*

The columns we want in the table for our exercise are sector name, ticker, industry average revenue growth, and company revenue growth. Currently, the Tickernomics tables feature allows only numeric columns, so sector and ticker will be in the row headers. Therefore, the total number of columns is 3, but only 2 of them are numeric, and one is the row header column (i.e., the first column of each row). The number of rows is the same as the number of outliers so we will need to determine this number as we go through all the companies and store it in the variable called outlierNumber. We will also need to create a comma-separated list of row headers containing the ticker names for each row. We will call this variable tickerCommaList. We will name the table IndustryRevenueGrowthAlphaMales. Here is the command to create the table:

```
CreateTable("IndustryRevenueGrowthAlphaMales", 2, outlierNumber,
    "Avg Revenue Growth,Revenue Growth",
    tickerCommaList,"my list of industry winners")
```

Before we begin coding we should learn about arrays that contain more arrays in each of their items. Let's remember Lego bricks again. Imagine you have a pile of Lego bricks and this time you also have a number of empty buckets. So instead of lining up the bricks that you pick from the pile you throw them in buckets based on the brick kind. So you are trying to be more organized this time.

The buckets should have a sticker label to identify the type of bricks it stores, otherwise it will be hard to know which bucket you need to place the brick in. It is also useful when you want to know which bucket to take the right kind of bricks from. Now the buckets are your initial array. So you first have an array of buckets and not bricks. Then each bucket is an array. It contains a certain number of bricks in each bucket.

Take a look at the picture below and think about it for a

moment. It is very important to understand this concept.

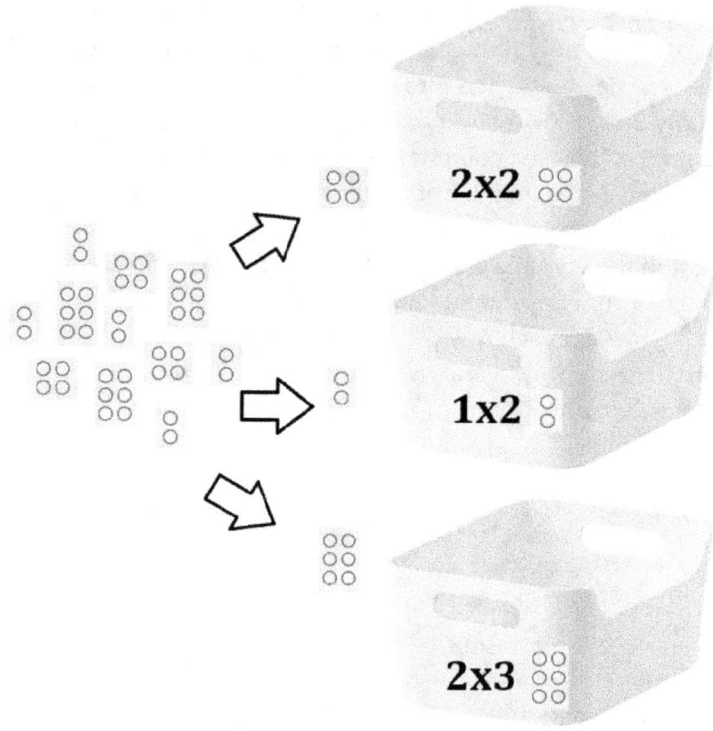

It would look something like this in code:

```
local buckets={};
buckets["2x2"]={"brick1","brick4"};
buckets["1x2"]={"brick3","brick6","brick7"};
buckets["2x3"]={"brick2","brick5"};
```

Then, to get the string for brick 5 you would use code like this:

```
local brick5Text=buckets["2x3"][2]
```

So you first get the correct bucket using the 2x3 key and

then you get the "brick5" string at position two in the array of bricks.

Let's change the third for-loop that we used previously to print outliers and instead record all outliers into a new array of arrays. We will call the new array of arrays "outliers". Each record in this array of arrays is another array that contains the following information: ticker, sector, avg revenue growth, and company revenue growth. This is all the information that we will need to transfer to the table later on. Here is the code to build an outlier array of arrays:

```
end -- end second loop where we store averages

local outliers={}
for i=0,GetTickerCount(),1 do
    local ticker=GetTickerByIndex(i)
    local sector = GetCompanyPropStr(ticker,"Sector")
    local revenueNow=GetXBRL(ticker,today,"","mmRevenueTTM")
    local revenuePast=GetXBRL(ticker,past,"","mmRevenueTTM")
    if revenuePast > 0 then
        local revenueChange=100*(revenueNow-revenuePast)/revenuePast
        if math.abs(revenueChange) < 300 then
            local industryAvg=industries[sector]
            local outlierPercent=revenueChange-industryAvg
            if outlierPercent>100 then
                --record the new array into outliers array of arrays at ticker key
                outliers[ticker]={sector,industryAvg,math.floor(revenueChange)}
            end
        end
    end
end -- end of the third loop where we search outliers
```

After this loop ends, the outliers array will have items stored at indices corresponding to their tickers and containing three pieces of information stored at positions 1, 2, 3: sector, industry avg, and revenue change for the ticker.

The next loop will build the row labels and also figure out the total number of outliers using tablelength command:

```
local outlierNumber = tablelength(outliers)
local tickerCommaList=""
for key,valueArr in pairs(outliers) do
    if tickerCommaList~="" then
        tickerCommaList=tickerCommaList .. ","
    end
    tickerCommaList=tickerCommaList .. valueArr[1] .. "/" .. key
end
```

"tickerCommaList" variable stores a text string that will become a comma-separated list of tickers separated by "/" with their corresponding sectors. Notice we use the ~= operator which translates as "not equal". We use it to append commas only when there are already items in the tickerCommaList text variable. We also use "/" as a separation between the sector name and the ticker.

It is time to add the final chunk of code to actually create the table and set values to each of the table cells. We also call the DeleteTable command first to delete the table with a such name if there is one to clean up previous old data from the last time the script was executed and generate the new data if such exists.

```
DeleteTable("IndustryRevenueGrowthAlphaMales")
CreateTable("IndustryRevenueGrowthAlphaMales", 2, outlierNumber,
    "Avg Revenue Growth,Revenue Growth",
    tickerCommaList,"my list of industry winners")

local row=0;
for key,valueArr in pairs(outliers) do
    SetTableValue("IndustryRevenueGrowthAlphaMales",0,row,valueArr[2])
    SetTableValue("IndustryRevenueGrowthAlphaMales",1,row,valueArr[3])
    row=row+1
end
```

The key command in this code is SetTableValue. It takes the table name in which to set the value ("IndustryRevenueGrowthAlphaMales") and then it takes column and row indices to which to set the value. The last argument is the value itself. Notice we also increment the row variable with every iteration of this for-loop (row=row+1) so we would set the values for the next rows in the table. Once this code runs we can admire our result in the Insight Table menu:

Script Tables   Custom Tables

Table Name: IndustryRevenueGrowthAlphaMales

Name	Avg Revenue ...		Revenue Growth
Financial Services/ONB	-11	105	
Industrials/SIDU	8	158	
Energy/CIVI	30	235	
Healthcare/BOLT	2	135	
Energy/NRT	30	159	
Healthcare/VBIV	2	124	
Consumer Cyclical/LCID	5	177	
Technology/OTMO	4	122	
Healthcare/OMGA	2	117	
Healthcare/NVOS	2	113	

This table will be available for a few hours and if you want to keep it permanently, you can do so by calling the StoreTable command: StoreTable("IndustryRevenueGrowthAlphaMales"). You can then load this table at any time in the future with the LoadTable command: LoadTable("IndustryRevenueGrowthAlphaMales"). You can also click the Export To Excel button to export the table to Excel.

10
MACRO TRENDS AND CUSTOM CHARTS

Growing up as an engineer, I was excited about the ability to calculate and predict how things will behave. Calculus dealt with motion in the physical world, easily simulating pretty much anything, from a spinning wheel to an electric circuit driving a train. All was well understood and clear; the books were written and almost unchanged since the 1970s. Then I learned about macroeconomics, and that changed everything in my worldview. There was a branch of science that openly admitted that a solution to accurately predict the economic system didn't exist.

You can try to predict things in economics, but calculus doesn't work very well in extremely complex systems full of rational and irrational decision-makers. My engineering mind desired the ability to predict how the system would work. I needed a well-defined solution, a book that could explain to me which formulas to use and which numbers to put into those formulas to get the answer. I was so used to clearly defined and well-tested solutions from my engineering studies that the economy seemed mysterious and exciting. There were no books that gave the solution, there were no formulas to predict it all.

Until AI picks up, the best machine to deal with complex incalculable systems is our brain. The brain evolved to act "rationally" in a complex environment with loosely defined rules. The brain needs a bit of help though. Our brains evolved to solve a lot of problems visually because we primarily interacted with the world visually. I know there are some people out there who are good without visuals, but for us, mere mortals, visuals help us perceive problems and solve them. Charts are extremely effective in providing visual help for our economic analysis. Scripts can help us a lot in building custom charts that will guide our complex decision-making.

Tickernomics has a lot of charts, but it is not possible to have all the charts out there predefined. So in this chapter we will learn how to build custom charts using scripting and how to mix corporate and macroeconomic data to uncover unique insights.

When you hear about the 9% annual dividend yield of a company today, do you get excited? I personally do! What about a 9% annual dividend yield in the year 1981? Do you think it was a good deal as well back then? No! It is a horrible deal because back then a 3-month treasury bill would give me 15% annually! Imagine that! 15% risk-free! So this little exercise teaches us one important thing: a company's economic parameters cannot be compared at different years without taking into account macroeconomic parameters at those different times.

Let's build a custom chart. Let's pick one of the dividend payers out there like MMM (3M Co) and build a chart of the relative dividend yield over the 10-year time period. The relative dividend yield will be calculated as a difference between the company's dividend yield and Federal Reserve's 10-year note yield every week during the 10 year time frame. This chart will help us visually understand if MMM actually increases its dividend yield relative to the "general cost of money". I like to compare various yields to 10-year treasuries because it is the closest thing to a risk-free yield that is available out there, and one of the most popular government bond types. If you build a stable income portfolio then dividend companies always compete with bonds for yield, and if a government bond can yield more than company dividends then the bond becomes quite attractive. Of course, bonds have serious drawbacks because if the economy goes through intense inflation then money might seriously drop in value over a longer time frame and bonds might be unattractive, even if they yield a lot. So even though government bonds are generally regarded as "risk-free", the possibility of inflation eroding your dollars' purchasing power is a real risk. I am bringing up this argument to indicate that nothing is simple in the economy and you need to think about a lot of factors.

Let's start with coding. First, we need to understand how to traverse the 10-year time period. I already explained that the system addresses time via day offset either from today into the past or from the "start of the times" forward (e.g. offset of -10 means that we are looking 10 days back). Currently, Tickernomics has the start of times as the year 2012, so it gives us roughly 10 years till now where I am writing this book in early 2023. So the offset of zero is somewhere in 2012. Let's write the for-loop that will traverse this time frame until today, skipping every 7 days because we do not need such high precision to have everyday data points calculated. We should be good at calculating one day a week. Here is the for-loop (in this for loop day will increment from zero until GetTodayDay() number with 7 days per each iteration):

```
function run()
  for day=0,GetTodayDay(),7 do
  end
end
```

The next step is to get 3M's TTM dividend yield for every day in the loop. We should also do the same for the 10 year treasury yield. Here is the code to do that:

```
local mmmDiv=GetXBRL("MMM", day, "", "mmDividendYield")
local treasuryYield=GetSourceValue("fred_dgs10",day)
```

Notice that we use GetXBRL to get the corporate data, but to get the macroeconomic data we use GetSourceValue call. GetSourceValue pulls data from various macroeconomic sources. FRED is the Federal Reserve. Another macro source is Treasury. You can find many dozens of data sources from GDP to Velocity of Money. DGS10 corresponds to 10-year treasuries.

These names sound cryptic but that is what the Federal Reserve likes to use in their system, so Tickernomics uses the same.

Since we mentioned GDP and the Velocity of Money, I would like to mention a very important macroeconomic equation – the equation of exchange:

$$M*V=I*P$$

M – money in the system
V – money velocity
I - inflation
P – GDP

This is a simplified definition, but it is good enough to give you intuition. M represents all the money in the system (usually we include not just actual dollar bills but also electronic money and money equivalents such as deposit certificates). V is money velocity which defines how many times on average one dollar changes hands during one year. It is an important parameter because if people keep money in a safe and never release it to the world then money velocity is zero and the world doesn't get any money, making money very "valuable". The opposite is also true and if people try to get rid of money as soon as they get it then money becomes artificially abundant. Inflation and GDP I hope you should be familiar with.

This equation holds true in a stabilized system and it doesn't hold when fast transient processes occur. Since transient processes are happening all the time in the system, I like to say that the equation is never holding. Jokes aside though this beautifully simple equation gives a sense of where the economic system is going as it moves through the transient process.

This equation visually gives a good sense of what will

happen if one of the components changes. For example, if someone increases the M volume then something on the right side might also increase to make the equation hold and often it is the I (inflation). On the other hand, if the economy is booming then GDP might grow a lot and if M and V stay the same then deflation might occur to keep the equation true. The most exciting parameter in this equation is money velocity. It is defined as the speed with which money changes hands. That is, if you buy something and you give the money to a shop, the shop owner might decide to either hold the money or immediately buy something with that money. The more such transactions occur in a year, on average, the higher the money velocity will be. Money velocity played a lot of tricks on economists in the past. One of the most powerful effects money velocity can do is to boost inflation. That is what happened in the 1980s hyperinflation. If people expect high inflation, guess what they will do with the money that they receive? People will try to get rid of the money as fast as possible because they expect high inflation. That makes money velocity increase and if you look at the equation above you can see that if the federal reserve issues a lot of new money and people expect high inflation because of that, then you can foresee that both M and V will increase at the same time and if GDP does not also grow, then inflation can increase dramatically. Interesting, right?

Let's get back to the chart building. To build a chart we use the SetPropByDay command. It takes the name of the chart, the day number, and the value. It is that simple. Here is how the code for our chart building looks:

```
for day=500,GetTodayDay(),30 do
  local mmmDiv=GetXBRL("MMM", day, "", "mmDividendYield")
  local treasuryYield=GetSourceValue("fred_dgs10",day)
  SetPropByDay("MMMRelativeDividendYield", day, mmmDiv-treasuryYield)
```

After you run this code you can go to the Insight Charts menu and you can find the MMMRelativeDividendYield chart. You can also use StoreByDayValue and LoadByDayValue commands to store the chart permanently and load it from the permanent storage. Here is the chart:

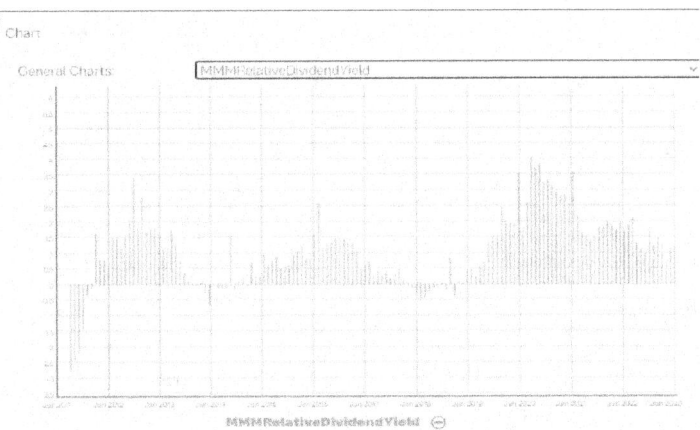

Notice that MMM's relative yield was negative in 2018. Probably was not the best choice back then for income.

Mixing macro and corporate charts can be a very creative and interesting task. Another useful correlation would be in comparing changes in government defense spending and changes in defense companies' revenue. Studying this relationship could allow you to predict how a defense company's revenue would be impacted by changes in government policy surrounding defense spending by observing the historical relationship.

Let's pick Lockheed Martin (LMT) as a defense company to research. We will calculate its revenue increases/decreases over the last 5 years. We will also build the government defense spending increases/decreases in percent over the same 5-year period. Comparing these two charts can give us a good feel about LMT's dependence on government contracts. Then we will do the same for General Dynamics (GD). Comparing GD and LMT in relation to government spending will give us a sense of which one is more dependent on government contracts.

Here is the code to do that:

```
for day=500,GetTodayDay(),30 do
    local lmtRev=GetXBRL("LMT", day, "", "mmRevenueTTM")
    local lmtRevPast=GetXBRL("LMT", day-365, "", "mmRevenueTTM")
    local lmtRevChange=math.floor(100*(lmtRev-lmtRevPast)/lmtRevPast)
    local gdRev=GetXBRL("GD", day, "", "mmRevenueTTM")
    local gdRevPast=GetXBRL("GD", day-365, "", "mmRevenueTTM")
    local gdRevChange=math.floor(100*(gdRev-gdRevPast)/gdRevPast)
    local defenceSpend=GetSourceValue("treasury_defensespending",day)
    local defenceSpendPast=GetSourceValue("treasury_defensespending",day-365)
    local defenceSpendChange=math.floor(100*(defenceSpend-defenceSpendPast)/defenceSpendPast)
    SetPropByDay("LMTRevenueChange", day, lmtRevChange)
    SetPropByDay("GDRevenueChange", day, gdRevChange)
    SetPropByDay("DefenceSpendingChange", day, defenceSpendChange)
end
```

The following charts will help us understand a bit more about defense companies. You are ready to create your own charts now!

Here are the three charts generated by the script (notice the huge spike in the last quarter due to war in Ukraine, also LMT seems to be more dependent on government spending as we can see LMT jumps and falls more with government spending jumps/falls compared to GD):

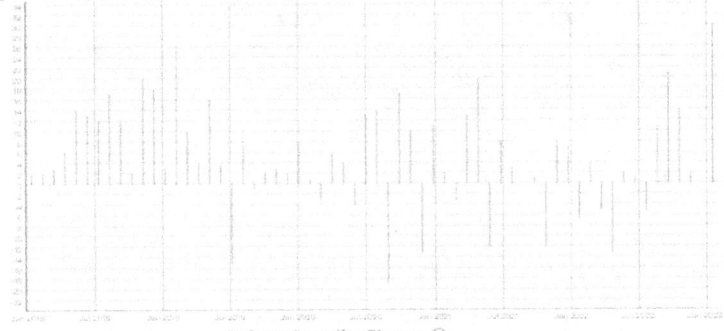

DefenceSpendingChange ⊖

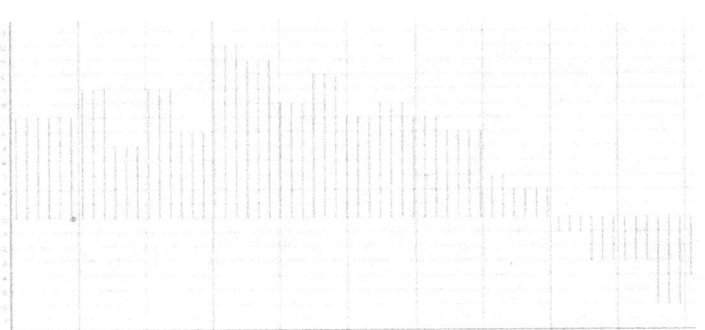

LMTRevenueChange ⊖

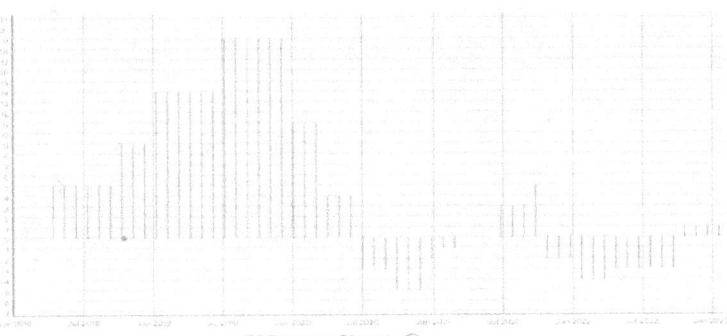

GDRevenueChange ⊖

What about other types of charts? We can build deep insights into various correlations between parameters by plotting them via scatter charts. Here is the example of the script building a scatter plot showing ROIC vs PS Ratio for all TSX listed stocks. The values shown for PS are as of the most recent market close day, and for ROIC they are as of the most recent quarterly filing(You can find this script on Tickernomics website. It is called ScatterPlotROICvsPS).

```
function run()
    DeleteGenericChart("TSX Stocks ROIC vs PS")
    DeleteGenericChart("TSX Stocks ROIC vs PS")

    local sum=0;
    local tickerTotal=GetTickerCount()
    for i=0,tickerTotal,1
    do
      local ticker=GetTickerByIndex(i)
      local Exchange=GetCompanyPropStr(ticker,"Exchange")
      if (Exchange=="TO") then
        local ROIC = GetXBRLLatest(ticker,"","mmROIC")
        local PS = GetXBRLLatest(ticker,"","mmPS")
        if ROIC<1000 and PS<80 then
        SetGenericChartPoint("TSX Stocks ROIC vs PS","S1",ROIC,PS,ticker)
        end
      end --if exchange
    end --ends for i=0

  SetGenericChartPropByName("TSX Stocks ROIC vs PS","XTitle","ROIC")|
  SetGenericChartPropByName("TSX Stocks ROIC vs PS","YTitle","PS Ratio")
  PrintLn("Go to Insight Charts > Generic Plots to see chart")
end
```

The result looks like this:

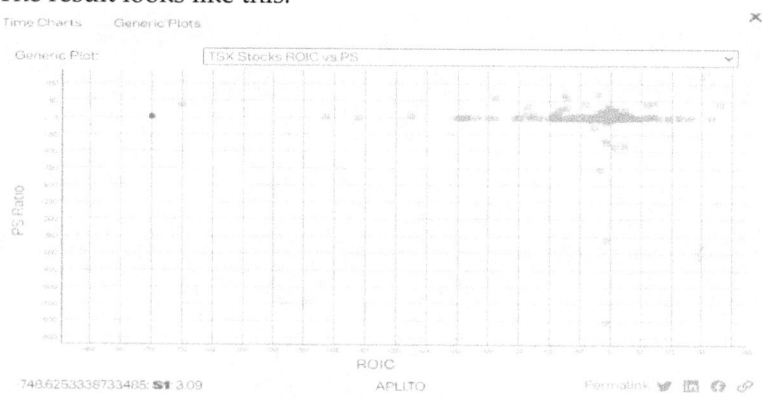

11
CIGAR BUTTS SCREENING

We are quickly moving towards boldly trying various investing strategies and building stock screeners using scripts. Stock screening is extremely popular among stock pickers. There are many websites with very powerful stock screening tools, yet they will never be able to match the screening power of scripting, as coding allows for unlimited flexibility in your screening techniques. We will start simple though.

In this chapter, we will describe the two popular strategies and explain how to create them in scripts. The more advanced screening strategies will be described in Chapter 23 and Chapter 24. Please, note that the strategies described in this chapter are only included because of their popularity and not necessarily because they are good strategies. The purpose of this chapter is, again, to show you what is possible so you can use these lessons to explore your own investing strategies that you may be interested in. Another important point regarding all investing strategies is that while they may have been good in the past, there is no guarantee that they will be effective in the future. The reason why they might become ineffective in the future lies in the Game Theory principles explained in Chapter 4. The main purpose of this chapter is to teach you to create strategies from scratch so you can learn how to build your own strategies as well as script-based screeners.

We will start with the Cigar Butt strategy. It is also called deep value strategy or Net Net stocks strategy. This is one of the most well-known stock investing approaches. It was popularized by Benjamin Graham as well as by other big names in investing as Warren Buffet, Charlie Munger, David Dreman, John Neff and Peter Cundill have all used this strategy in the past. The key idea is to find profoundly undervalued companies. They should be so undervalued that the entire capitalization of the company should be less than the current assets of the company minus all the liabilities of the company (both current and noncurrent). The logic for this investing approach is that if the company were to shut down tomorrow and sold all its assets you would still get back more than you invested. Capitalization is the total sale price of the company, it is like a house's total sale price. Continuing the house analogy, you calculate everything that the house is worth and subtract any liens the house might have and you still end up with the house's assets (roof, floors, walls, electrics, etc.) being worth more than the selling price of the house. Wouldn't you want to buy it?

You might think that there are no such companies out there, but it turns out there are plenty of companies that have a capitalization less than current assets minus all liabilities. It is because current assets often include items that cannot be easily sold, or because the company is losing money so quickly that you will end up having nothing pretty soon, or sometimes creative accounting results in such cigar butt conditions. So once you build the list of cigar butt companies take a closer look at them to learn why they are so cheap.

Here is the whole script to print out Cigar Butt stocks:

```
function run()
    local c=GetTickerCount()
    for i=0,c-1 do
      local ticker=GetTickerByIndex(i)
      local CurrentAssets=GetXBRLLatest(ticker,"","AssetsCurrent")
      local Liabilities=GetXBRLLatest(ticker,"","Liabilities")
      local MarketCap=GetXBRLLatest(ticker,"","mmCapitalization")
      local Name=GetCompanyPropStr(ticker,"Name")
      local country=GetCompanyPropStr(ticker,"Country")
      if country=="United States" then
        if CurrentAssets>10 and Liabilities>10 and MarketCap>10 then
          if (CurrentAssets - Liabilities)>MarketCap then
              PrintLn(ticker .. "  " .. Name)
          end
        end
      end
    end
end
```

As you can see, we pull the three key characteristics of the company: Current Assets, Total Liabilities, and capitalization. Then we filter out any non-US companies for easier apples-to-apples comparison and we also filter out companies that have less than 10 million in the three characteristics in order to get rid of tiny oddballs or garbage. Then we filter for Cigar Butts with this if-then statement:

```
if (CurrentAssets - Liabilities)>MarketCap then
```

The output looks like this:

```
2023-01-31 02:43:31: BXMT  BLACKSTONE MORTGAGE TRUST INC.
2023-01-31 02:43:31: BXSL  Blackstone Secured Lending Fund
2023-01-31 02:43:31: OPEN  Opendoor Technologies Inc.
2023-01-31 02:43:31: PSEC  PROSPECT CAPITAL CORP
2023-01-31 02:43:31: MDC  M.D.C. HOLDINGS INC.
2023-01-31 02:43:31: GBDC  GOLUB CAPITAL BDC Inc.
2023-01-31 02:43:31: EQRX  EQRx Inc.
2023-01-31 02:43:31: PEB  Pebblebrook Hotel Trust
```

If we pick the OPEN ticker for example, we will notice

that this company is a classic case of cigar butt stock since it has lost money for a long time. Skipping various funds in the list, the other operating company in this list is EQRX which is, you guessed it, a biotech company. Those beasts are so hard to value! Biotechs keep researching something and one day might turn out to be a billion-dollar unicorn, but of course most of the time they just slowly die out. So the best thing the reader can do is to either improve filtering in your script further to filter out funds, biotechs, and money losers, and maybe if you are lucky you can find something truly valuable. The script is published on Tickernomics so you can copy it to your workspace and play with it further. I encourage that.

Another popular screening algorithm I want to target in this chapter is called Altman-Z Score. This technique tries to predict if the company is heading for bankruptcy. The reason I placed this algorithm in the same chapter with the Cigar Butts screener is that I believe it is a very good idea to creatively combine Altman-Z Score with the Cigar Butts screener because you are looking for edgy companies among Cigar Butts and Altman-Z Score counterweights those by giving you a score of how likely the company goes bust. So a potentially promising pick can be a Cigar Butt company with a good Altman-Z Score.

The Altman-Z Score paper was published in 1968 by Edward Altman, a Professor of Finance at New York University. Altman used to teach "Bankruptcy and Reorganization" and "Credit Risk Management" at the Stern School of Business. So the guy knew what he was building into that formula pretty well. The formula became very popular later on. Let's look at the formula to understand the reasons why it might be a good predictor of bankruptcy probability:

$$ZScore = 1.2{*}A + 1.4{*}B + 3.3{*}C + 0.6{*}D + 1{*}E$$

Where:

```
A=WorkingCapital/TotalAssets
B=RetainedEarnings/TotalAssets
C=EBIT/TotalAssets
D=MarketCap/TotalLiabilities
E=Revenue/TotalAssets
```

The coefficients 1.2;1.4;3.3;0.6;1 are empirical and represent the art and skill of Mr. Altman. Let's look at each of the components individually:

A – represents the liquid assets that the company has at its disposal. It is important to understand that certain types of companies have huge plants and expensive equipment just because they are in some capital intensive industry, so those companies naturally will have A very low compared to some IT consulting companies for example as those would have almost no illiquid assets. If you had read my previous chapters you noticed that I advocate avoiding flat-screening all companies as equals but instead screen companies within their respective domains, comparing apples-to-apples if possible.

B - reflects the company's profitability, age, and earning power. Companies that do not distribute profits (through dividends) accumulate their profits into the retained earnings account on the balance sheet. Companies that lose money for a long time will have retained earnings very low or even negative.

C – is very similar to B except it is the ratio of the current earnings so it reflects what is going on right now, unlike B which represents what happened with the earnings in the past.

D – represents the ratio of a company's price to its liabilities and can have a high value **only** if the market (which is often actually right) perceives the company as stable (a company with a high market cap relative to liabilities is unlikely to face solvency issues).

E – this factor is very sensitive to the industry of the company. For example, Amazon will have enormous revenues and relatively small assets as a lot of selling happens in the cloud these days, while a research company in the biotech space won't have sales but will have some expensive equipment registered as assets. How can you compare those? The intention of this factor is to determine if a company uses its assets efficiently to actually bring in some revenue.

According to Altman, a score below 1.1 indicates a company heading into a bankruptcy risk zone. So now, once you scan for Cigar Butts and once you identify some companies that you like. Why don't you create a script that calculates their Altman-Z scores just to make sure you are not buying a company that will go bust soon? The code below will calculate the Altman-Z score:

```
---Enter ticker here ->
function run(ticker)
  local CurrentAssets=GetXBRLLatest(ticker,"","AssetsCurrent")
  local CurrentLiabilities=GetXBRLLatest(ticker,"","LiabilitiesCurrent")
  WorkingCapital = CurrentAssets-CurrentLiabilities

  local TotalAssets=GetXBRLLatest(ticker,"","Assets")
  local TotalLiabilities=GetXBRLLatest(ticker,"","Liabilities")
  local RetainedEarnings=GetXBRLLatest(ticker,"",
    "RetainedEarningsAccumulatedDeficit")
  local MarketCap=GetXBRLLatest(ticker,"","mmCapitalization")
  local Revenue=GetXBRLLatest(ticker,"","mmRevenue")
  local EBIT=GetXBRLLatest(ticker,"","OperatingIncomeLoss")

  A=WorkingCapital/TotalAssets
  B=RetainedEarnings/TotalAssets
  C=EBIT/TotalAssets
  D=MarketCap/TotalLiabilities
  E=Revenue/TotalAssets

  ZScore = 1.2*A+1.4*B+3.3*C+0.6*D+1*E

  PrintLn("Altman Z-Score for this company is: "..ZScore)
end
```

As you can see the script doesn't look that difficult and uses all the commands you already used before. The one new thing that you probably noticed is the argument "ticker" in the "run()", as well as the comment "Enter ticker here". This is a technique that allows Tickernomics to show the user an option to enter data (such as a ticker) that will be used in the execution of the script, very convenient!

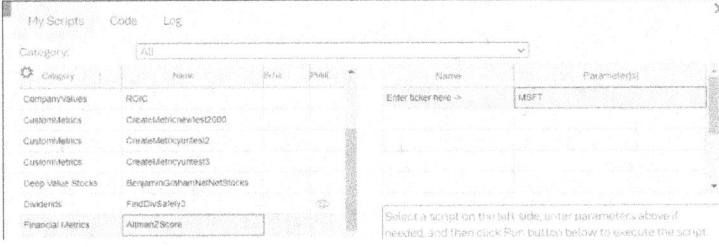

12
PORTFOLIO BASICS

I want to take a pause from exploring the stock-picking algorithms and talk about portfolio building instead. We will return to stock picking in later chapters. This book is not intended for day traders and algorithmic high-frequency traders. This book is written by a regular DIY investor who has a day job and is looking to invest in stocks and build a strong portfolio over time. That is why the book is called Algorithmic Investing and not Algorithmic Trading. The purpose of the book is to help investors make smarter investments and also help with portfolio rebalancing from time to time. There is obviously a huge difference in how investing is approached in such cases when the intention is to do just a few transactions per month or per quarter instead of doing continuous trading daily.

Another important point to understand is that your primary task is not to pick stocks, but to build a portfolio that is right for you! Professional financial advisors will ask you a lot about your life goals, your risk tolerance, etc. Mathematically though, the only important parameter an investor needs to consider when building a portfolio is risk tolerance. How much are you prepared to lose in the worst-case scenario? An investor's life's targets do not play an important role because it is obvious that a portfolio should maximize return and the only limiting factor is risk tolerance.

In this chapter, we will look at the important portfolio characteristics that can be used to statistically understand your portfolio: alpha and beta. Other characteristics will be described in the next chapters: standard deviation, VaR, Sharpe ratio, and Sortino ratio. In later chapters, we will learn how to calculate them and how to properly balance the portfolio. Let's start with understanding the investing process in the context of portfolio building.

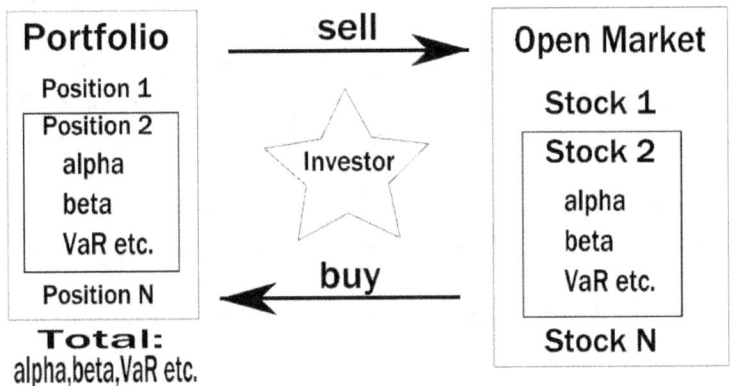

An investor executes transactions to buy stocks and to sell stocks. Each stock/position has its own alpha, beta, VaR, and other properties. The overall portfolio will have a combined alpha, beta, VaR, etc. composed of all its positions and their weights. A position weight is just the percentage a particular position takes in the whole portfolio. So as you can see every buy/sell transaction will change your portfolio alpha, beta, VaR, and other parameters. So when you consider a stock pick you cannot just look at that stock as an isolated decision (let me buy this stock because I like its current price and PE). You actually should consider your current portfolio characteristics and how they change after you buy the stock. Besides mathematical risk and performance measures (alpha, beta, VaR, etc) the portfolio also has a somewhat related but still separate measure – diversification. We will learn how to take into account all these parameters when stock picking and when considering a position reduction or a sale. Finally, it is important to take into account that usually a transaction to buy/sell is not free because of taxes and fees in general for buying and selling. This expense creates a small barrier to initiating a transaction in the first place.

Firstly, let's clearly understand alpha and beta. Alpha is the measure of the return superiority of an asset compared to the market reference. It sounds a bit cryptic so I will try to explain with an example. Let's say we want to measure the alpha of AAPL stock. We need to pick a reference. For stocks, we usually pick S&P 500 returns as a reference. So the total return of AAPL minus the total return of our reference (S&P 500) will give us AAPL's return superiority (which is similar to alpha; alpha accounts for risk as shown later). The next natural question to ask is over which time period should we measure the returns? It can be one year, five years or ten years, or honestly any other time frame. I think measuring alpha over 10 years could provide us with the most useful insight. On Tickernomics, you can see the total return for a stock in the "Companies" option on the Ratios tab. Here is what we see for AAPL:

What about the S&P500? You can use the SPY ticker to get the return for it. It is important to note that Total Return includes the appreciation of the value of the assets as well as dividends that are reinvested (AAPL does pay dividends). Unfortunately, SPY won't include the dividends, which cannot be ignored. So let's instead measure a stock's CAGR return and compare the two between AAPL and SPY. Wait. What is CAGR? If we want a "simple" return for an asset for a certain period, we take the initial price and the end price and then do the following calculation:

$$100 \frac{\text{EndPrice-StartPrice}}{\text{StartPrice}} \%$$

This calculation does not take into account the reinvesting of the profits of an asset annually. So CAGR will take care of that as its abbreviation literally says that: Compound Annual Growth Rate (It is very similar to the compounding of interests). Here is the CAGR formula:

$$100\left(\left(\frac{\text{EndPrice}}{\text{StartPrice}}\right)^{\frac{1}{n}}-1\right)$$

(n is the number of periods - usually the number of years)

You can see the CAGR of a stock in the Summary tab above the chart and it is calculated for the currently selected period:

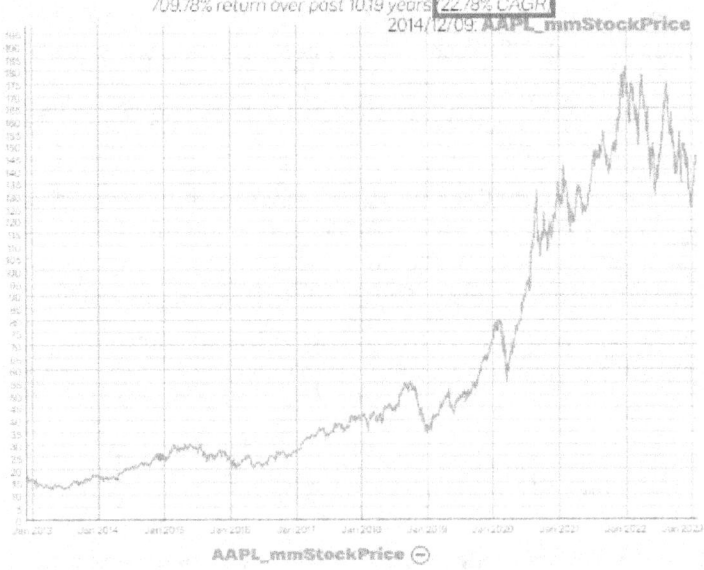

AAPL_mmStockPrice ⊖

SPY has a CAGR of 13%. So AAPL's return superiority with given above assumptions is 22%-13%=9%. That is very good!

Let's calculate the actual alpha for AAPL, but first, we need to understand beta, which is an extremely important parameter too.

Beta measures an asset's return correlation with the reference's return. The reference for stocks is again the S&P 500. So a stock that has a beta equal to 1 had the return same to S&P500's return. For example when the S&P 500 had gained 2%, the stock had also gained 2%, similar if the S&P 500 loses 2%, the stock has lost 2%. A stock that has beta between zero and one will have the return curve move along with the S&P500 return curve but it will be less aggressive, meaning if S&P500 return spikes up then your stock's return will typically not go as high, but the good news is when S&P500 plunges then your stock won't plunge as much. If the beta is above 1 then the stock return still moves along the S&P500 return but in a more aggressive way. For example, if the stock has a beta of 2 then when S&P500 has a return of 20% then your stock will have a return of 40%, but if S&P500 has a bad year and it is negative 15% then your stock will have -30% plunge that year. Finally, if the stock has a beta below zero then it means that the stock's return moves in the opposite direction of the S&P500, and when the return goes up for S&P500 then your stock's return would typically go down and vice versa. There are very few such stocks, one example is biotech stock HGEN. Overall, the higher the absolute value of beta the higher the risk.

We can calculate alpha now that beta is understood. Here is the formula to calculate the asset's alpha:

alpha=actual return - beta*market return

The market return is usually the return of the S&P500.

We can see that alpha is the extra return we get above the expectation based on the stock's beta and S&P500 performance. It is important to understand that both alpha and beta are properties of each individual stock, but alpha and beta are also properties of a whole portfolio since you can add up weighted components of the portfolio together to obtain the portfolio's total alpha and beta.

Every money manager is scared of alpha being low or negative because alpha is used by investors to measure money managers' performance. Money managers have to build a portfolio with positive alpha for their customers. otherwise why would a customer go to a money manager and pay fees? It would make sense for customers to just invest in the S&P500 which has an alpha of essentially zero:

alphaSP500=SP500ActualReturn-1*SP500AvgReturn=0

We will continue the exploration of proper portfolio building in the next chapter.

13
PORTFOLIO ANALYSIS

If alpha measures performance and beta measures risk then why would you need more parameters for your portfolio? The short answer: these two numbers do not give a full picture of your portfolio's construction. I personally use standard deviation and VaR. We will address the standard deviation in this chapter. VaR will be described in the next chapter and I will include the Sharpe ratio, and Sortino ratio as well because I know other people love to use those. Let's start with the standard deviation.

Standard deviation is widely used in science, engineering, economics, and math. You may have studied it in school, and all it does is give a good sense of how volatile whatever is being measured is. The primary measure of your portfolio is its total value. The total price of your portfolio changes daily. How much does it change? Sometimes a lot and sometimes a little, so the standard deviation can capture that in a single value to give you a sense of your portfolio's volatility. Here is the formula for standard deviation:

$$\sqrt{\frac{\sum_{i=1}^{n}\left(X_i - X_{mean}\right)^2}{n-1}}$$

n – is the number of measurements
Xi – the specific measurement and Xmean is the mean of all measurements.

The mean is calculated as the sum of all measurements divided by the number of measurements. So essentially the average.

The measurement for the portfolio is just its total price

on a specific date. So we can do such measurements for a year every single day and that should give us a pretty good value of the standard deviation for our portfolio. Obviously, it is also possible to get a standard deviation for a specific stock or an index such as S&P500. You often hear in the news the other name for standard deviation – volatility. So if you didn't know, now you know how to calculate it manually.

Let's say you get a specific number for standard deviation. How can it be used? If, for example, the mean price of your portfolio is 50 (in the chart below, 50 is the midpoint for the price axis), then here are three possible values for standard deviation rendered as a distribution of days when the price was between 0 and 100 on the price axis:

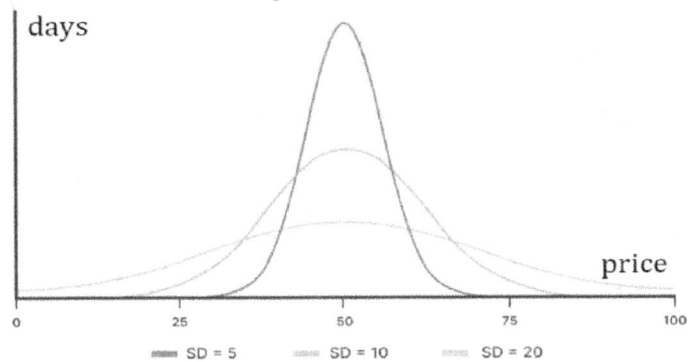

As you can see the absolute majority of days the price was between 30 and 60 for the blue line which has the lowest deviation. But the yellow line with deviation 20 shows that there were plenty of days when the price was below 25 and above 75. Because the yellow line has a much larger range of prices, it is more volatile and thus has a higher standard deviation (SD = 20). This should give you a good intuition of what the standard deviation number means.

Let's create a demo portfolio in Tickernomics and then write a script to calculate its overall standard deviation.

Standard deviation will give us the specific number identifying how much in dollars on average our portfolio value fluctuates. Beta only gives us the volatility relative to the benchmark of S&P500 but standard deviation gives us an expected dollar amounts we are projected to fluctuate by historically. Later you will learn that standard deviation is the primary tool used in investing banking to measure risk of your portfolio. To create a portfolio in Tickernomics you should go to the Portfolio and click Transactions button first and enter various purchase transactions. Then you can see your resulting portfolio.

Let's start our script with a for-loop that will go through your portfolio positions and print them on a screen. The below screenshot also includes brief explanations stating what each line of code is doing:

```
function run()
  local today=GetDayAsString(GetTodayDay());
  CalcPortfolioStats("2020-01-01",today) --from 2020 till today
  local positionCount=GetPositionCount()-1
  for j=0,positionCount-1,1  do
   local ticker=GetPositionTicker(j)
   local remainQty=GetPositionValue(j,"EndPeriodTotalQty")
   if  remainQty > 0 then
     --print only "live" positions
     local totalReturn=GetPositionValue(j,"TotalReturnSinceBought")
     PrintLn(ticker .. " " .. math.floor(remainQty) .. "  " ..
          math.floor(totalReturn) .. "%")
   end
  end
end
```

The most tricky command to understand here is CalcPortfolioStats. It takes two parameters. The first parameter is the date from which to calculate statistics for your portfolio. For example, a specific position's return is time-dependent: do you want a return for 3 months, for one year, or from the time the position was established? The second parameter is the date when the calculation ends. This is quite a unique feature because it allows calculating stats such as a return for a specific period in the past.

Another tricky command is GetDayAsString. We use it to convert the today's day number to a readable date text(or programmers call text a string), because CalcPortfolioStats takes only readable date strings as input parameters. Once the statistics for the portfolio is calculated we go through a pretty standard for-loop iterating through each portfolio position. GetPositionTicker retrieves the ticker for a position using an index of the position as an input parameter. An index is an order in which this position is present in the portfolio.

Finally, GetPositionValue retrieves a specific named parameter of the position. It is a powerful command since it can retrieve a lot of a position's stats. As an example, we retrieve and then print the position quantity of remaining stocks as well as the return of the position for the period in the script above. Notice we use the remaining qty(remainQty) check to be more than zero to filter out closed positions(a closed position would have no stocks left so remainQty will be zero).

Here is the output of this script:

```
2023-02-03 01:42:32: SEB 4  8%
2023-02-03 01:42:32: SNY 128  52%
2023-02-03 01:42:32: TAP 70  -9%
2023-02-03 01:42:32: TKC 700  35%
2023-02-03 01:42:32: TU 220  3%
2023-02-03 01:42:32: VZ 55  -5%
2023-02-03 01:42:32: WM 100  24%
```

Tickernomics has a specialized value for standard deviation which is called spVariance. It is the square of the monthly standard deviation of a stock's return. If you have taken a statistics class before, you may recall that Variance = standard deviation squared. So to convert that to normal annual return standard deviation measured in percent you need to take the square root of spVariance and then multiply by 12 to convert to annual and then also multiply by 100 to convert to percent. We will modify the script above to go through portfolio positions and then we will use the GetXBRLLatest command with the spVariance parameter to extract the standard deviation for each position. Once that is done we can then calculate the weighted average deviation of the whole portfolio. We can use GetPositionValue with the PositionPercent parameter to get the position weights. I hope the weighted average formula is something everyone knows:

$$\bar{x} = \frac{w_1 x_1 + w_2 x_2 + w_3 x_3 + \cdots + w_i x_i + \cdots + w_n x_n}{w_1 + w_2 + w_3 + \cdots + w_i + \cdots + w_n} = \frac{\sum_{i=1}^{n} w_i x_i}{\sum_{i=1}^{n} w_i}$$

Here is the code to calculate your portfolio's standard deviation from weighted average of its positions:

```
function run()
    local today=GetDayAsString(GetTodayDay());
    CalcPortfolioStats("2020-01-01",today) --from 2020 till today
    local positionCount=GetPositionCount()-1
    local avgVariance=0
    for j=0,positionCount-1,1  do
     local ticker=GetPositionTicker(j)
     local variance=GetXBRLLatest(ticker,"","spVariance")
     local annualVariancePercent=math.sqrt(variance*12)*100
     local remainQty=GetPositionValue(j,"EndPeriodTotalQty")
     if  remainQty > 0 then
       --print only "live" positions
       local positionWeight=GetPositionValue(j,"PositionPercent")
       avgVariance = avgVariance + annualVariancePercent*positionWeight
       PrintLn(ticker .. "  " .. positionWeight .. "   " .. annualVariancePercent)
     end
    end
    PrintLn("Portfolio Variance: " .. avgVariance)
end
```

And here is the output:

```
RIO 0.078915214330053  26.759733686353
RTX 0.032808989110588  27.573596788243
SEB 0.048497450537069  22.957442502503
SNY 0.01893092824004  20.071267213858
TAP 0.010952800079589  29.290164458164
TKC 0.01086739812965  38.595015473776
TU 0.014319466948943  17.59656125927
VZ 0.00681751566079  17.279440740385
WM 0.046547112786022  19.248817288252
Portfolio Variance: 28.023168172377
```

As you can see we print out each position's weight in the
portfolio as well as its variance. We also print out the total
variance of the portfolio.

14
EVEN MORE PORTFOLIO ANALYSIS

Alpha, beta, and standard deviation are very useful parameters, but my favorite parameter to analyze the portfolio risk is VaR. It stands for Value at Risk. If you watched the movie "Margin Call", another movie about the Great Recession of 2008, then you might notice that the main character discovers a model that predicts the financial downfall of the company. That model was based on VaR analysis! The company that is not named in the movie is most likely Goldman Sachs. Given Goldman Sachs' actions during 2008 and taking into account that Goldman survived 2008 pretty well, we can clearly see how important VaR analysis is to understand your exposure to risk that even movies mention it

VaR allows you to live a happy life as an investor, because if you know that VaR for your portfolio shows that the maximum you can realistically lose is something around 15% of everything you own then it is not scary to you as an investor and not going to be life-changing and you can watch the news in the world unfolding from a safe distance so to speak.

The VaR parameter is not a single number but a few numbers that require detailed explanation. In plain English, VaR analysis answers a simple question: How much will you lose in the worst-case **realistic** scenario? The keyword here is "realistic", because VaR is not interested in crazy one-in-a-billion probability when things go extremely bad all at once, yet it still addresses very unlikely, but still **realistic** cases of when a lot of your positions go bad at once.

Now let's look at the visual intuitive representation of what VaR tries to calculate:

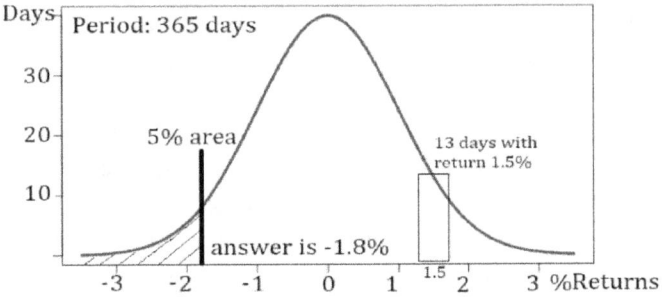

Imagine you measure your daily portfolio return over a period of one year. You add each day to the chart above at X value corresponding to that day's return. For example, you will accumulate 13 days with a daily return of 1.5% during a year. Most days will be unremarkable and your daily portfolio return will be close to zero, therefore most days will be close to where X = zero. Hence the curve is highest at zero. This is a neutral year so the portfolio doesn't gain much or lose much. VaR has two input parameters: a period of measurement (in our case 1 year) and the percentage of days with the worst returns (out of all days in the time period, what percentage of days with the worst returns do you want to consider, in our case we picked 5%, so we are interested in the 5% of days with the worst returns). 5% equals the hatched area under the curve, while the area under the whole curve corresponds to all 365 days in a year.

If you didn't understand the two input parameters, please reread the paragraph above, otherwise, you will not understand the output parameter of the VaR analysis. The output parameter is: At least how much my portfolio decreases in value in the chosen percentage of the days during the chosen period of time. The answer in the chart above is 1.8%. So my portfolio will lose **at least** 1.8% on 5% of the days during the 1 year period. So VaR gives you a feel for how much exposure you might be having in absolute dollar amounts. So during this neutral year and since your portfolio composition is neutral as well, you won't lose that much even in the worst 5% days of the year. Many pick 1% instead of 5% for VaR because then they can see what the worst of the worst days' losses can be.

Calculating VaR the academic way involves too many naive assumptions and the need to calculate covariance. I will explain what covariance is, but I will not give you an academic method of calculating VaR, because it is a bit mathematically complex. Instead, we will explore a much more intuitive and robust method called the Monte Carlo method. The Monte Carlo method uses random numbers to calculate something that is hard to devise a formula for.

We learned about variance (a deviation from the mean) in the previous chapter and it is time to understand covariance now. As "co" implies it is a variance correlation between two entities. Why are some portfolios "good" and some are "bad"? It is not just the returns, but also the risk that counts. The bad event might not hit a risky portfolio and it would show amazing returns, until one day when the "bad" does eventually hit the portfolio. So reducing the risk of the portfolio is a paramount task. The most common way of building resilience into a portfolio is diversification. The mathematical way to measure diversification is a covariance matrix, which is a table showing the covariance between each component of a portfolio:

	A	B	C
A	0.4	0.5	0.2
B	0.5	0.01	-0.3
C	0.2	-0.3	0.9

Let's look closer at this matrix. Let's say A is a pipe making company, B is an oil giant, and C is a small tech startup. The untrained eye cannot catch much in this matrix, but let's first look at AxA, BxB, and CxC of the covariance matrix. Those are squared variances of A, B, and C. You can see that B has extremely low variance because it is an oil giant and we saw very little change recently in oil prices. C has a very high variance because it is a small tech startup. Let's look at AxB and BxA cells. They are the same numbers, and it is true for AxC, CxA, and BxC, CxB. These cells show relationships among each of the stocks. The AxC relationship has a smaller number than AxB. It is true that a pipe maker's stock price is less correlated with a tech startup's stock price than with the oil giant stock price, which might be building pipelines to supply oil. Finally, BxC has a negative number and indeed it is often the case that when the stock price of oil companies goes down the stock price of tech companies goes up. The negative correlation is at the core of building stable portfolios that can withstand so-called "rotations". A rotation is when investors rotate from one class of stocks into another (e.g. from cyclical into growth, or from growth into income stocks).

A covariance matrix should be built to calculate VaR analytically. A covariance matrix is hard to build because you need to be able to understand the ever-unique relationship between every other stock in your portfolio and over a certain period. That is why often it is easier to use the Monte Carlo method to calculate the VaR of a portfolio realistically.

In order to understand the Monte Carlo method, let's first understand how this same method is used to find infinitely precise PI values. We all know PI = "3.1416 and so on and on and on". What is the area of a square of size 1? It is 1 because Square Area=1x1. What is the area of a circle touching all 4 sides of such a square?
Circle Area = PI*Diameter/4. Diameter is 1 of such a circle, so

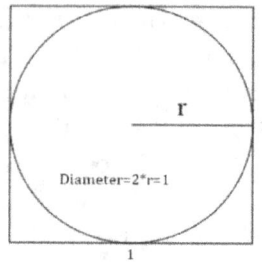

Circle Area=PI/4. The ratio of a circle area to square is:

$$\frac{\bigcirc \text{Area}}{\square \text{Area}} = \frac{\frac{1}{4}\pi}{1} = \frac{1}{4}\pi = \text{ratio}$$

Imagine you do a drawing of that square and circle, then put it on a wall and start throwing darts into the drawing, taking note of whether the dart hit the circle or not. After you did it for a while the ratio of darts hitting the circle to the total darts thrown will be roughly equal to 1/4th of PI. Moreover, the more darts are thrown the more precise the PI value will be calculated. This is the essence of the Monte Carlo method: use randomness to find values otherwise hard to find, and the more you do it the more precise you are gonna get. Lua has a function to get a random value: math.rand(start range, end range). It will give you a random number every time you call it in a range [start range, end range]. So for example if your start range is 5 and your end range is 10 then the random number will be between 5 and 10, so 5, or 6, or 7, or 8, or 9, or 10.

Here is the program that throws random "darts" 100 times and gives you the PI estimate:

```
local steps=0
local hits=0
while(steps<1000) do
    --random number between 0 and 999
    local X=math.random(-1000,1000)
    local Y=math.random(-1000,1000)
    local radius=math.sqrt(X*X+Y*Y)
    if radius <= 1000 then
        hits = hits + 1
    end
    steps = steps + 1
end
PrintLn("PI= " .. 4*hits/steps)
```

Here is the output for 1000 steps:

PI= 3.112

If we increase steps to 10000, we get this output:

PI= 3.140188

The program is very simple. We find X and Y coordinate randomly between -1000 and 1000 which will define a random "dart throw". We find the distance from 0,0 to the dart throw point using Pythagorean Theorem. Please note, the math.sqrt function calculates a square root of a number. The condition of whether the dart hit the circle is elementary geometry: the distance should be equal to or less than the radius:

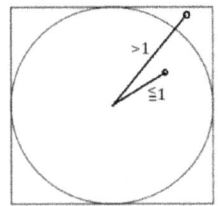

Now armed with this knowledge you are ready to apply Monte Carlo to your portfolio in order to find an approximation of VaR. We will use a simplified version of the Monte Carlo simulation because it can get complicated really fast. We will not track the price of the stock changes day-by-day over a time frame that proper Monte Carlo portfolio simulation does, we will not use stock properties either, but only the variance of the stock to identify how much the stock typically fluctuates. For simplicity of demonstration, we will run the simulation a number of times (365*100 to be exact to simulate 365 days and 100 ways the changes might have turned out) and for each of those days we will take in the value the stock fluctuate randomly off its initial value. The algorithm will remember the largest absolute loss of the portfolio and print it at the end. This a rough approximation of the real VaR algorithm, but still, it is useful information to see how resilient our portfolio is.

The code has the first for-loop that repeats 36500 times and within this loop, the other loop goes through every position in the portfolio and calculates random fluctuation from the original value. We sum up every position's fluctuation together and this gives us a whole portfolio of one-day fluctuation. Since we do that randomly 36500 times we will sometimes get a coincidental large negative fluctuation of multiple positions at the same time. This huge loss will be recorded and then printed after all loops are finished running. Here is the code for the whole Monte Carlo simulation:

```
local today=GetDayAsString(GetTodayDay());
CalcPortfolioStats("2020-01-01",today) --from 2020 till today
local positionCount=GetPositionCount()-1
local maxLoss=0
for days=0,365*100,1 do -- run random attempts a lot
  local portfolioLoss=0
  for j=0,positionCount-1,1  do
      local ticker=GetPositionTicker(j)
      local varianceMonthlySq=GetXBRLLatest(ticker,"","spVariance")
      local varianceDaily=math.sqrt(varianceMonthlySq*12)/365
      -- assume stock can change at most 300 times of its avg daily change
      local varianceAssumed=varianceDaily*300
      local remainQty=GetPositionValue(j,"EndPeriodTotalQty")
      if  remainQty > 0 then
          --print only "live" positions
          local positionPrice=GetPositionValue(j,"EndPeriodTotalPrice")
          local dailyFluctuationMaxUSD=math.ceil(varianceAssumed*positionPrice)
          -- random fluctuation from +-dailyFluctuationMaxUSD
          local dailyFluctuation = math.random(-dailyFluctuationMaxUSD,
                                    dailyFluctuationMaxUSD)
          portfolioLoss = portfolioLoss + dailyFluctuation
      end --if
  end --for j
  if portfolioLoss < maxLoss then
    maxLoss = portfolioLoss --record the largest loss
  end
end -- for day
PrintLn("Max Loss:" .. maxLoss)
```

This is a cool little piece of code because it actually gives us some expectation of what we might lose and it naturally takes into account each stock's variation. Unfortunately, this method is just the start and it doesn't take any covariance into account. So the next natural step to improve this code is to at least account for the industries the stocks are in, as well as track the daily stock price changes for a full year.

Let's briefly touch on two other popular parameters to measure risk: the Sharpe ratio and the Sortino ratio.

$$\text{Sharpe Ratio} = \frac{\text{Expected Return - Risk Free Return}}{\text{Standard Deviation}}$$

The Risk-Free Rate is usually what US treasuries can give you as a return (the 10-year rate is typically used). The

Expected Return is the expected return of whatever you are calculating Sharpe Ratio for, e.g. 10% could be an expected return of an Apple stock you just bought. The Sharpe Ratio gives you a sense of your portfolio performance while taking risk into account. It can get negative if your portfolio yields less than treasuries. It can get positive but very small when Standard Deviation is very high, which would be in the case of a risky portfolio. Notice how the top part of the equation gets higher if the return is high, but the bottom part gets higher if risk (as measured by standard deviation) increases. So the best portfolio is when the top part grows, but the bottom part doesn't. That is when the ratio is getting really high. The Sharpe ratio between 1 and 2 is considered good. A ratio between 2 and 3 is very good, and any result higher than 3 is excellent. A high Sharpe ratio indicates higher returns with disproportionately lower levels of risk, which is a highly desired outcome in investing.

The Sortino ratio has the exact same formula as the Sharpe ratio except the standard deviation is only calculated for the downside. So just replacing standard deviation with downside standard deviation in Sharpe ratio formula we will get the Sortino ratio. This ratio is considered better suited to give the investor a sense of the risk in the portfolio since we only consider the loss fluctuation part of the ratio. Think of it this way: the fluctuations in the direction of improving return reflect how much variation the "good" times have, and the fluctuations in the direction of return decreases reflect the "bad" times for the asset and those bad times is what Sortino ratio captures, completely ignoring how the good times fluctuate. So if you are interested in the risk during bad times then Sortino is your friend.

15
WATCH LIST

I don't know about you, but I cannot survive in today's fast-moving world without my phone's reminder app. It is very hard to keep track of things happening during my busy days. What about keeping track of things happening in the entire world economy? The daily news is one way of staying up-to-date, and there are many resources out there to stay up-to-date with the news, but do you consider "news" when the revenue of a company you care about suddenly drops by 20% quarter-over-quarter? We will learn how to build lists of companies that we care about manually and using scripting, we will also learn how to get those notifications similar to those I get on my phone's reminder app.

Watchlists can be helpful in following way:

- Treat your watchlist as a single place of your thoughts and interests in the field of investing that you once recorded.
- A reminder utility similar to reminder apps on your phone
- An alarm utility to notify you when the price of a stock becomes attractive
- A single place to organize your sticky notes and build a checklist for your investments

Let's say you are interested in AMZN and you want to know when this stock drops in price by 10% from its 200-day moving average. If you go to the Watch List menu in Tickernomics and add AMZN manually then the only option in the UI is to be notified when the daily price drops below the target price. This is not what we want because we want to dollar-cost average into AMZN and buy it in chunks long-term. So setting a new target price is too much hassle. Especially if you plan to use the "stock drops in price 10% from its 200-day moving average" rule for many other stocks in your watch list. So the solution to this task is to write a small helper script. The script will go through the stocks on your watch list and apply the "stock drops in price 10% from its 200-day moving average" rule, and if a stock satisfies the rule we will spawn a notification.

First, we need to learn how to iterate through a watch list in scripts. Watch list positions are considered a special kind of Transaction. It is a transaction of type zero. You have commands to get the number of your transactions (GetTransactionCount) as well as to read a property of a transaction (GetTransactionValue and GetTransactionValueStr). When you read a property of a transaction you need a unique ID of that transaction. We will use the command GetTransationIdFromIndex to convert the sequential index of a transaction in the list to its ID.

Here is the code to print all your watches:

```
function run()
    local transCount = GetTransactionCount()
    for i=0,transCount-1,1 do
        local transID=GetTransactionIdFromIndex(i)
        local transType=GetTransactionValue(transID,"TransactionType")
        --print only watches
        if transType==0 then
            local ticker=GetTransactionValueStr(transID,"Ticker")
            PrintLn("Watch for " .. ticker)
        end
    end
end
```

I got this printout:

2023-02-06 23:53:44: Script output:
2023-02-06 23:53:44: Watch for AMZN

As you can see we can add watches manually through

122

the Tickernomics Watchlist UI and then we can run a script that can traverse all your watchlist picks. We can set up this script to run weekly by clicking the Schedule button in the My Scripts main tab. So your script will run periodically.

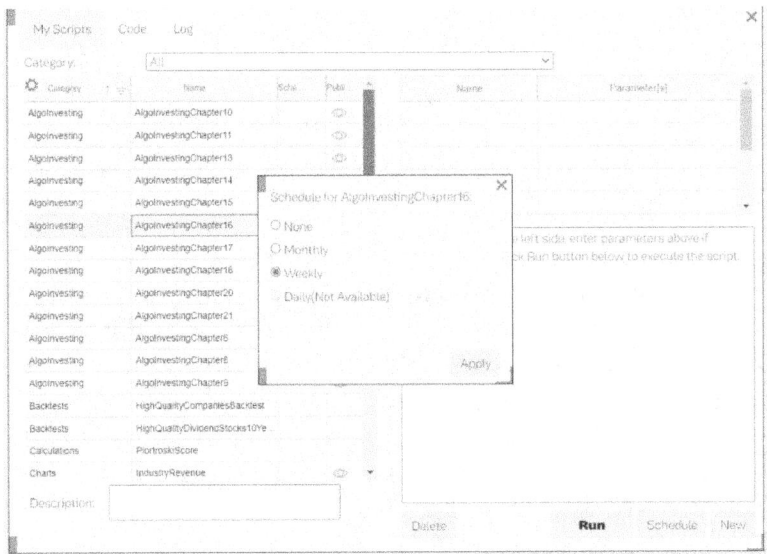

The only part left is to modify this script to do something useful. Let's add TSLA to the watch list as well. In our case, we want to identify a significant decrease in the stock price (AMZN or TSLA) by 10% from the 200 day running average. If you don't know what the running average is, don't worry, it is very simple. It is what the name implies. Imagine you have a stock price recorded for every day for 200 days. The average price during these 200 days (sum up prices of all 200 days and divide by 200) gives us the running average price for today. Then tomorrow comes and you have a history of stock prices for 201 days. The running average for tomorrow will be 200 days average counting back from tomorrow. This will continue as the timeline moves forward. So running average gives us a smoother price curve:

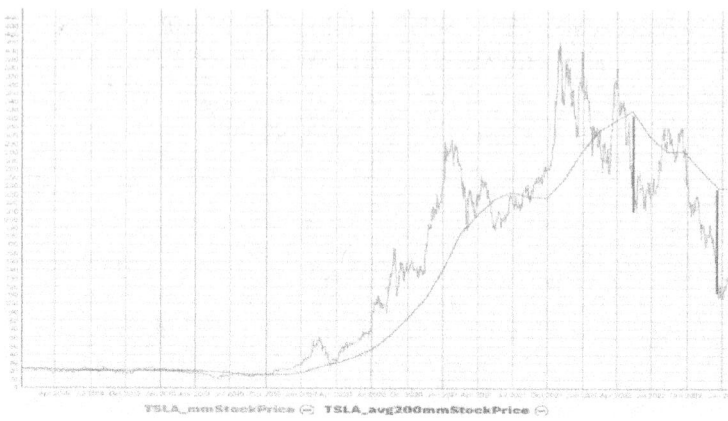

The two >10% deviations of TSLA stock price from its running average give us the opportunity of buying the stock so later you can either sell it or hold it (if that is what your strategy entails). Of course, each case is unique and there are many factors to take into account, but at least it would be useful to get notified when a stock drops a lot relative to its average as you indicated an interest in such a stock by placing it into a watch list.

We need to learn a new command to send a notification – AddAlert. This command takes just one argument which will be the text to display. It is different from PrintLn, because it doesn't print it into a log but pops up a message box on the screen, so you won't miss it. Remember that the script will run regularly using the scheduler so you won't even run the script manually, so the popup is essential to get notified when using the scheduler. The popup might not appear immediately, but it will pop up within a minute or so.

Here is the code to get the notification when a stock from the watch list deviates by 10% or more from the running average:

```
local transCount = GetTransactionCount()
for i=0,transCount-1,1 do
    local transID=GetTransactionIdFromIndex(i)
    local transType=GetTransactionValue(transID,"TransactionType")
    --print only watches
    if transType==0 then
        local ticker=GetTransactionValueStr(transID,"Ticker")
        local stockPrice=GetXBRLLatest(ticker,"","mmStockPrice")
        local avgStockPrice=GetXBRLLatest(ticker,"","avg200mmStockPrice")
        if stockPrice>0 and avgStockPrice>0 and
                            (1.1*stockPrice) < avgStockPrice then

            AddAlert("Price 10% less than avg: " .. ticker .. " ".. 
                stockPrice .. " " .. avgStockPrice)


        end
    end
end
```

And here is what you get on your screen:

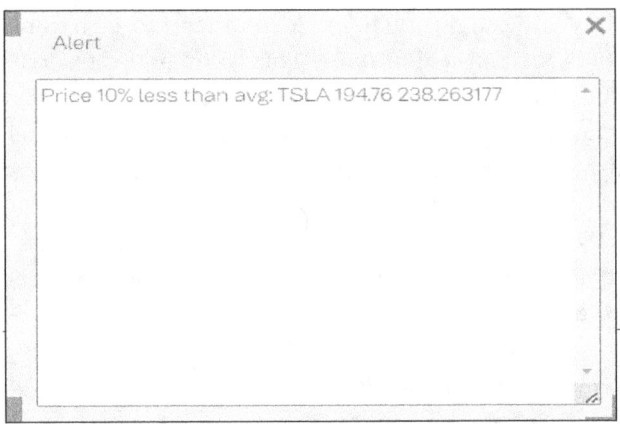

Of course, this is a very basic demo and you can develop your own sophisticated conditions for when you want to be notified. The conditions can take into account revenue changes, debt changes, changes in valuation metrics and so on, not just the price change. It also can be a combination of conditions that uniquely trigger the alarm. That is what I call an art of investing.

We learned how to trigger alarms for your watch list that you built yourself. What if you wrote a script to build the actual watch list too, so you wouldn't even need to do manual entries into the watch list? Let's learn how to do this. We will fixate on the banking industry, and we will add watches automatically for the companies that have gained 30% in revenue when compared to 400 days running average for Revenue. This can help us identify banks that have recently seen a spike in revenue and it prompts us to investigate why that is. You need to be careful with this kind of script or you might flood your watch list with too many entries and it will be hard to manage. So let's start with scripting and learn the commands to create a watch list entry.

An entry in the watch list is a kind of transaction with type zero. Transactions are also used to build a portfolio. There can be buy and sell transactions. A command to set a transaction property is SetTransactionValue. This command can set many transaction properties. The type of transaction can be set by the TransactionType property. As I said, the value zero means it is a watchlist transaction, type 1 means it is a buy, and type 2 means it is a sell. SetTransactionValue command takes the transaction unique ID as the first argument; the name of a transaction property as the second argument; and a value of that property as the third argument.

Here is how to create a watch list entry:

```
SetTransactionValue(0,'TransactionType',0)
SetTransactionValueStr(0,'Ticker',"MSFT")
SetTransactionValue(0,'UnitPrice',300)
SetTransactionValueStr(0,'Note',"I want MSFT to be 300")
local trId=StoreTransaction(0)
PrintLn(trId)
```

Since we created a new watch, we use zero as the transaction ID. Once the properties of the watchlist entry have been set, calling StoreTransaction(0) will create a new transaction with all the above values. StoreTransaction will return a new transaction ID which will be unique for this watch This transaction id can then be used to call other transaction/watch functions later.. You can later use it to modify the watch like so:

```
local note = GetTransactionValueStr(trId,'Note');
SetTransactionValueStr(trId,'Note',note.."!")
StoreTransaction(trId)
```

This code retrieves the Note property of the watchlist entry identified by the trId unique ID. Then we set the Note property again, appending the exclamation sign at the end of the note.

Here is the final code that will auto-generate new watches for banks that gained 30% in revenue compared to 400-day running average:

```
function run()
    for i=1,GetTickerCount()-1 do
      local ticker=GetTickerByIndex(i)
      local industry=GetCompanyPropStr(ticker,"Industry")
      if StartsWith(industry, "Banks") then
          local revenue = GetXBRLLatest(ticker,"","mmRevenue")
          local revenueAvg = GetXBRLLatest(ticker,"","avg400mmRevenue")
          if (revenue>0) and (revenueAvg>0) and (revenue>(1.3*revenueAvg)) then
              SetTransactionValue(0,'TransactionType',0)--watch
              SetTransactionValueStr(0,'Ticker',ticker)
              SetTransactionValue(0,"UnitPrice",0)
              StoreTransaction(0)
          end
      end
    end
end
```

BACKTESTING INTRO

Backtesting is one of the most popular techniques to evaluate investment strategies. Once you have a strategy to test, you apply it in the past years and see how it performed until today. Let's take the simplest strategy to test: buy and hold a position in a stock that dropped more than 50% from its running average, yet its revenue didn't drop. The idea behind this is that a stock that dropped significantly despite seeing no real decline in revenue may have dropped just due to fear or some news. And by taking advantage of a depressed stock price for a business that has not fundamentally changed, we may see above average returns. We will buy a few such positions every month for 10 years starting from 2012 and hold until today. We will see the performance of such a portfolio and compare it to the S&P500 performance, which is the most popular benchmark.

It is sometimes believed that if backtesting demonstrated good results for a certain strategy, then such a strategy should perform well in the future. This is not always the case, because of the Game Theory effects we discussed earlier in the book. Other players will employ this same strategy and it might not work anymore in the future. A good example of this is the so-called "Dogs of the Dow" strategy. It made Motley Fool famous. Dogs of the Dow is a stock-picking strategy devoted to selecting the highest dividend-paying Dow stocks and holding them for a year, then revisiting them. There are variations of this strategy. Backtesting of the strategy showed great results back then, but once the strategy became popular, it underperformed in the following years.

Backtesting has another problem. Some of the economic conditions are extremely long term and you cannot backtest a strategy properly, because the current macroeconomic conditions are unique enough to skew your strategy's performance. This factor is huge and often overlooked. Older people will tell you how different the 1960s felt compared to the 2000s. You can't enter the same river twice... It sounds poetic, but there is math behind all of this. Some factors are easier to measure and some are much harder. We do have historic inflation figures, average yields, unemployment levels, etc. Some factors are really hard to measure though: people are different, their aspirations and priorities are different, and families and consumer behaviors are different across generations. All these "invisible" factors do influence the economy, and eventually the performance of the investment strategy.

I mentioned a lot of problems with backtesting, however backtesting is still a useful exercise. I would say it is a perfect technique to test out your assumptions and theories about an investing method that you just came up with. How can you know if the idea you just had is good? Backtesting can provide a good starting point to test your idea on real data, even though that data is from the past and might not apply to the future, but if your idea is really good it has to perform somewhat decently in the past, otherwise, how can you risk investing with your idea in the future.

Finally the really smart investors out there are learning to account for changes in macroeconomic conditions and try to adjust the backtesting results for the future. For example, if the backtesting ran during times of low inflation and you live right now in times of high inflation then you can adjust by the inflation coefficient of some of your investing strategy formulas. So you could assume your strategy might work in a different environment just as well. Again, like I said before, to get good results you need to become an artist who strives to build a sophisticated and elegant strategy.

Let's write a backtesting script for the above-mentioned simple strategy: "buy and hold a position in a stock that dropped more than 50% from its running average yet its revenue didn't drop". We learned how to store a transaction in the previous chapter. Since we will build an experimental portfolio, I would recommend registering as a new experimental user on Tickernomics. Let's call this new user John Doe. The user should have no transactions and an empty portfolio.

Here is the code for the backtest:

```
local currentDay=GetTodayDay()-365*10 --10 years ago
local transactionDaysNumber=math.floor(365*9/30)
local alreadyBought={}
for i=0,transactionDaysNumber,1 do
  for j=1,GetTickerCount()-1 do
    local ticker=GetTickerByIndex(j)
    if alreadyBought[ticker] == nil then --check didnt buy before
      local curPrice=GetXBRL(ticker,currentDay,"","mmStockPrice")
      local avgPrice=GetXBRL(ticker,currentDay,"","avg400mmStockPrice")
      local curRevenue=GetXBRL(ticker,currentDay,"","mmRevenue")
      local avgRevenue=GetXBRL(ticker,currentDay,"","avg400mmRevenue")
      if curPrice>0 and avgPrice>0 and curRevenue>0 and avgRevenue>0 and
          ((1.5*curPrice) < avgPrice) and ((1.1*curRevenue) >= avgRevenue) then
        SetTransactionValue(0,"TransactionType",1) --buy
        SetTransactionValueStr(0,"TransactionDate",GetDayAsString(currentDay))
        SetTransactionValueStr(0,"Ticker",ticker)
        SetTransactionValue(0,"Qty",1)
        SetTransactionValue(0,"UnitPrice",curPrice)
        StoreTransaction(0)
        alreadyBought[ticker]=true --mark we bought it
        break  -- stop ticker loop cause we bought a stock for this month
      end
    end
  end -- loop through companies to find one to buy
  currentDay = currentDay + 30 -- move to next month
end -- main loop to do 1 transaction per month
```

"transactionDaysNumber" will calculate the total number of purchase transactions to execute during the whole time, so we take 365 days in a year, multiply by the year number (which is 9 in this case, since we are doing a 10 year backtest but need at least 1 year of historical data to calculate the 400 day moving average for revenue) and divide by 30 days in each month. This ensures we are purchasing one stock every 30 days. The rest of the code simply pulls the values for all the properties for our strategy using GetXBRL functions. Then we execute the strategy described above with the "if" statement.

If you go to Transactions menu you will see this:

Type	Date	Ticker	Qty	Unit Price	Total Price
Buy	2021-12-25	PINS	1	37.42	37.42
Buy	2021-11-25	ZM	1	206.3	206.30
Buy	2021-10-26	VIPS	1	12.46	12.46
Buy	2021-09-26	CPNG	1	26.31	26.31
Buy	2021-08-27	LU	1	8.2605	8.26
Buy	2021-07-28	PDD	1	79.53	79.53
Buy	2021-06-28	IRTC	1	67.32	67.32
Buy	2021-05-29	AFRM	1	60.81	60.81
Buy	2021-04-29	HAE	1	68.25	68.25
Buy	2021-03-30	RLX	1	10.67	10.67
Buy	2021-02-28	GLPG	1	82.6	82.60
Buy	2021-01-29	SRPT	1	90.13	90.13
Buy	2020-12-30	TXMD	1	59	29.00
Buy	2020-11-30	CVI	1	10.6351	10.64
Buy	2020-10-31	TEF	1	2.8019	2.80

And here is the Portfolio front page:

So our 10-year buy-and-hold portfolio has a total return of 134.8%. (Warning: Do not use this strategy yet! Read the next chapter to understand why.) The value of the portfolio grew from 3985 USD to 9353 USD. S&P500's SPY ticker today (02/02/2023) is 415 USD and 10 years ago it was 136 USD, which is a return of 415-136=205%. Also, we didn't account for dividends to simplify the example. So at first glance, it looks like the S&P500 outperformed our strategy, but in our backtest we didn't buy everything all at once 10 years ago, instead, we were buying one new stock every month during the whole period (one purchase of one individual share of stock per month). So we need to simulate that with SPY and buy 1 SPY ETF unit for every month and then calculate the overall return. I slightly modified the script above to do only SPY purchases. So buying 1 SPY per month for the last 10 years produced a 68% return:

✿ Ticker	Alloc%	Qty	Unit Price	Total Price	Gain	Gain%	Name
SPY	100	110	412.35	45358.5	18495.08	68.84	SPDR S&P 500 ...

See the script to produce SPY only 10 year portfolio on the next page:

```
local currentDay=GetTodayDay()-365*10 --10 years ago
local transactionDaysNumber=math.floor(365*9/30)
local alreadyBought={}
for i=0,transactionDaysNumber,1 do
  local ticker="SPY"
  local curPrice=GetXBRL(ticker,currentDay,"","mmStockPrice")
  SetTransactionValue(0,"TransactionType",1) --buy
  SetTransactionValueStr(0,"TransactionDate",GetDayAsString(currentDay))
  SetTransactionValueStr(0,"Ticker",ticker)
  SetTransactionValue(0,"Qty",1)
  SetTransactionValue(0,"UnitPrice",curPrice)
  StoreTransaction(0)
  currentDay = currentDay + 30 -- move to next month
end -- main loop to do 1 transaction per month
```

The result of this simple strategy seems to be not bad at all! Let's review how the backtesting script works.

The main outer loop increments the currentDay by 30 days starting with the date 10 years ago from your today's day. Then we run the inner loop to go through all the companies. We use the alreadyBought array to register a ticker that was bought previously. This is necessary to avoid buying the same company over and over again. Then we retrieve the stock price and revenue as well as their averages, followed by a gigantic if-then statement that ensures that indeed our price dropped a lot and revenue grew at least slightly. Then we create a transaction on currentDay with Qty (quantity) 1 for the selected ticker.

Since we buy different companies every month for 10 years we achieve significant diversification, which protects against exposure to specific failed companies. You can observe the industries on the pie charts in the Portfolio menu. Indeed you will see that many positions have a significant loss, but because many more positions had significant gains, the overall performance of the portfolio is good.

The one hidden danger of backtesting results is the so-called "survivor bias". We only test on companies that survived until today. So our backtest cannot buy a company that doesn't exist today since it is simply not on the list of companies. This is a common problem with backtesting as the results might be skewed to a more positive outlook simply because we are oblivious to all those companies that disappeared. According to data acquired by Finbold, a total of 179 companies have been delisted from the major United States exchanges between 2020 and 2021. In 2021, the number of companies on Nasdaq and the New York Stock Exchange (NYSE) stood at 6,000, dropping 2.89% from last year's figure of 6,179. In 2019, the listed companies stood at 5,454. Therefore, it is likely that the results of our backtest would have changed slightly if we had included these delisted companies. The other deceptive problem of backtesting is look-ahead bias. It is a problem of knowing if indeed all information we see now was available at specific time in the past.

Finally, the simple backtest above is not meeting the

quality standard at all because we had no randomization! So the result we have got is most likely misleading. The reason is very simple: we were choosing the first company that matched your criteria, but what if the list of companies is ordered based on implicit patterns (in fact I ran a randomization test later and discovered that if companies were picked randomly then the overall result was a negative return!). For good quality backtesting results we should pick companies at random or even better: pass the algorithm through all companies. We will see in the next chapter how a more realistic backtest should be done.

We have built a backtest with very little code and yet we enjoyed great visual analysis built-in into the Portfolio module of Tickernomics. Most of the backtesting is done in a different way though. There is very little UI present in backtesting systems. Also, creating a new portfolio with the new user account in Tickernomics just to see the resulting portfolio is too cumbersome. What if you want to run hundreds of backtests resulting in hundreds of test portfolios? Moreover, you probably noticed that the backtesting script took some time to run. That is because backtesting is usually extremely resource intensive. You will overload the system by creating all those testing portfolios. Many companies run backtests on supercomputers. We will step into a more professional, and more complex backtesting scenario in the next chapter.

17
REAL BACKTESTING

Honestly, we got "lucky" to observe a "good" return with the backtest in the previous chapter. Most likely it was a bias from how the companies were ordered in the for-loop. In this chapter, we will parse **all** companies and apply much more sophisticated conditions in order to achieve our objective of beating S&P500.

Backtesting can get complex and computationally expensive very fast, so you need to understand the limitations. We tried to apply a number of limiting factors to the backtest in the previous chapter. First of all, we only did one transaction per month for 10 years. If we decided to do it per day, our backtest would exceed the allowed time limit of 10 minutes to run a script on Tickernomics. Another way the algorithm was limited computationally is that we picked the first matching stock and bought it without checking all the stocks for each month. In this chapter, we will remove this second optimization so you will notice the algorithm runs longer but produces real results.

We will modify the previous backtest in a number of ways. First of all, we will buy the **best** choice and not just the **first** choice every single month. What is the best choice? Let's say it is the stock with the largest drop in its stock price between today and 2 months ago. The largest drop in the stock price would suggest that the sentiment is very low for the stock so it is trading very cheap. The revenue change will be analyzed relative to its 400 days running average where revenue from the most recent quarter must be at least 10% higher than the 400 days running average for quarterly revenue. The second change is that we will not generate a new transaction to avoid flooding the portfolio, but we will do a manual calculation of the return. This way the code will be faster and also will form the skeleton for any further improvements in backtesting. Furthermore, we will use much more sophisticated criteria for the "best choice".

To get the "best choice" we need to iterate through all tickers in the inner loop and store the best choice in a new bestTicker variable: Since we will not use transactions anymore we should still record them somewhere, so a new array is introduced that stores the ticker as the value and the day of purchase as the key.

The new loop is added after the main loop to evaluate the portfolio total gain percentage as well as to print the portfolio contents.

First, let me show to you the result of running the new backtest script, so you can see it beats the S&P500:

```
2023-02-09 13:11:46: SDG 2020-12-11 27.8957 20.41
2023-02-09 13:11:46: HCG.TO 2016-04-16 26.73177451
2023-02-09 13:11:46: PATK 2016-03-27 43.267 75.01
2023-02-09 13:11:46: CSIQ 2014-10-04 34.46 40.11
2023-02-09 13:11:46: CVEO 2017-12-27 29.16 35.79
2023-02-09 13:11:46: ODC 2015-11-08 24.9357 37.96
2023-02-09 13:11:46: CBD 2014-04-07 40.4385 3.53
2023-02-09 13:11:46: SEDG 2016-01-07 29.13 319.41
2023-02-09 13:11:46: HCA 2020-08-13 130.4285 255.2
2023-02-09 13:11:46: NEM 2015-02-01 21.8532 48.72
2023-02-09 13:11:46: SKY 2019-05-31 24.03 68.8
2023-02-09 13:11:46: NVCR 2020-09-02 84.68 92.43
2023-02-09 13:11:46: BIG 2020-06-14 32.1258 17.47
2023-02-09 13:11:46: GOOS.TO 2020-11-01 30.940501
2023-02-09 13:11:46: BBSI 2016-06-15 33.484 98.38
2023-02-09 13:11:46: TRGP 2020-12-31 25.4916 74.6
2023-02-09 13:11:46: 1219 2163 Return=77
```

In the results above, we print the ticker and price on the day it was purchased, and then we also print the price of today. 77% vs 68% is not such a huge advantage over SP500 but still it does seem to beat S&P500 in the last 10 years.

The full script source code is on the next page.

```
local currentDay=GetTodayDay()-365*10 --10 years ago
local transactionDaysNumber=math.floor(365*9/20)
local alreadyBought={}
local transactions={}
for i=0,transactionDaysNumber,1 do
  local bestTicker=""
  local bestRise=0
  for j=1,GetTickerCount()-1 do
    local ticker=GetTickerByIndex(j)
    if alreadyBought[ticker] == nil then --check didnt buy before
      local curPrice=GetXBRL(ticker,currentDay,"","mmStockPrice")
      local curDebt=GetXBRL(ticker,currentDay,"","mmDebt")
      local prevDebt=GetXBRL(ticker,currentDay-300,"","mmDebt")
      local curFCF=GetXBRL(ticker,currentDay,"","mmFCFTTM")
      local prevFCF=GetXBRL(ticker,currentDay-200,"","mmFCFTTM")
      local prevPrice=GetXBRL(ticker,currentDay-60,"","mmStockPrice")
      local avgPrice=GetXBRL(ticker,currentDay,"","avg400mmStockPrice")
      local curRevenue=GetXBRL(ticker,currentDay,"","mmRevenue")
      local avgRevenue=GetXBRL(ticker,currentDay,"","avg400mmRevenue")
      local cap=GetXBRL(ticker,currentDay,"","mmCapitalization")
      local industry=GetCompanyPropStr(ticker,"Industry")
      local country=GetCompanyPropStr(ticker,"Country")
      if cap>100 and curPrice>0 and prevPrice>0 and industry~="Biotechnology"
        and (avgPrice<500) and (avgPrice>20) and curDebt<prevDebt
        and avgPrice>0 and curRevenue>0 and avgRevenue>0
        and ((1.2*prevPrice) < avgPrice) and (prevFCF>0)
        and (curPrice > avgPrice) and (0.8*curFCF>prevFCF)
        and (curRevenue >= avgRevenue)
        then
          local risePrice=(curPrice-avgPrice)/avgPrice
          local riseFCF=(curFCF-prevFCF)/prevFCF
          local rise=risePrice+4*riseFCF
          if rise > bestRise then
            bestRise=rise
            bestTicker=ticker
          end
      end
    end
  end
  end -- loop through companies to find one to buy
  if bestTicker ~= "" then
    transactions[currentDay]=bestTicker
    alreadyBought[bestTicker]=true
  end
  currentDay = currentDay + 20 -- move to next month
end -- main loop to do 1 transaction per month
-- calculate return
local totalCost=0
local totalPrice=0
for kDay,vTicker in pairs(transactions) do
  local startPrice=GetXBRL(vTicker,kDay,"","mmStockPrice")
  local todayPrice=GetXBRLLatest(vTicker,"","mmStockPrice")
  PrintLn(vTicker .." " .. GetDayAsString(kDay) .." " ..
    startPrice .." " ..todayPrice)
  totalCost = totalCost + startPrice
  totalPrice = totalPrice + todayPrice
end
local returnPercent=math.floor(100*(totalPrice-totalCost)/totalCost)
PrintLn(math.floor(totalCost) .. " " .. math.floor(totalPrice) ..
  " Return=" .. returnPercent)
```

138

Take time to look through the code first and compare it to the previous chapter's backtest script. You should notice the first difference which is the transactions array. It is the array that will replace real transactions and will store them as day and ticker key-value pairs. Then you could notice the beginning of the first for-loop which iterates through the 10-year time period. Notice that the increment is slightly denser now: it is 20 days instead of 30 days. We need more options to choose from as we try to find the best choice instead of the first match. It is always better to have more options to choose from for the best choice.

We can also notice the two new variables: bestChoice and bestRise. They record the best stock choice and its total percentage rise of the rank. We can see how the rank is calculated (variable "rise") further in the code. It is a combination of price rise and FCF (free cash flow) rise. Notice we use the weight coefficient for FCF as 4. This is an empirically selected weight based on the experience of the author.

As we look inside the ticker selection for-loop we should notice a much larger number of various parameters pulled from the system for the ticker: FCF, revenue, stock price, debt, capitalization, and industry. The script above is still considered simple for a real-life backtesting strategy, but even this simple script is quite involved. The script also runs for almost a full 10 minutes of the allowed script running time.

As we look further into the script we can see a gigantic "if statement" that checks a multitude of conditions that must be satisfied for the ticker to become a candidate for purchase. Notice that Biotech companies are excluded from being a candidate, that is because they are almost impossible to value and the majority of them tend to have wild swings. They are sort of a "joker" card in investing.

If we look now at the last for-loop in the script, we

should notice the iteration of the transaction array which is summing up the prices of the stocks we purchased in the past and their current price. So we will obtain the total growth percentage from this information. Notice it will not include anything about dividends, which can be hard to ignore in many cases.

As you can see, the real backtesting script is much more involved but the return it produces is much closer to reality. The fact that we considered all the stocks every 20 days for 10 years allows us to obtain quite reliable statistics on this strategy. It is also less impressive compared to the naive backtest from the previous chapter, but it is always better to know the bitter truth than the sweet lies. A lot of backtests I have seen make a mistake of just picking one point in time to buy many stocks and stick with those stocks. This approach is flawed because maybe at that specific time, the market was in the decline state, so almost any strategy would have performed great as the overall market climbed out of that low. Yet other backtests make the mistake of not considering all stocks but a small subset which can also skew the strategy's real performance.

One way to improve backtesting is to call GetTickerCount(true) instead of just GetTickerCount(). This way you will get not just the tickers of actively traded companies but also the tickers of all the delisted companies in the past decade or so. This way you can resolve the problem of "survivorship bias". It is very important to account for those companies that disappeared otherwise your backtesting results can be too optimistic!

Backtesting is a very efficient technique to know what to buy, and until now we were putting all our efforts into stock picking, but what about selling? Let's say we finally accumulated a large portfolio, so how do we know what to sell and when? We will learn about this subject in the next two chapters.

SORTING

Before we develop algorithms for selling we need to learn how to sort things in code. We will be improving the dividend stock-picking algorithm we developed in earlier chapters (Chapter 7: Looking For Stable Dividends). If you don't remember that algorithm, please review the chapter again. The essence of the algorithm was to traverse every stock and calculate a rank from 5 parameters: dividend yield, revenue growth, debt to capital, capitalization, and outstanding shares growth. If the rank was more than 1, then we would print out such stocks.

This was a useful algorithm, but what if there are too many stocks printed? How can you manually select the only one you want to buy out of hundreds? Sorting can help a lot. We can order the matched stocks based on rank, printing the highest-ranked stocks first. So you then could look at the supposedly best matches. I said "supposedly" for a reason. The best-ranked stock is almost never your best choice. We need to look at a myriad of other factors to consider a stock for investment, so the ranked list only provides us a good pre-selected list of candidates.

Tickernomics has a command to do sorting of an array:

```
getKeysSortedByValue(setarray, function) returns sorted key list from key-value input setarray
{}. The second argument is a function which can be used for sorting:
getKeysSortedByValue(arr, function(a, b) return a > b end)
```

This is probably the hardest command to understand so we will take it slow. If you read the description of the command it is probably very difficult to understand what it does... Let's start with the arguments. It has two arguments. The first argument is an array. The second argument is something called "function". Before we understand "function" lets us first look at a little program where getKeysSortedByValue is used:

```
function run()
    local companyAssets={}
    companyAssets["MMM"]=46000
    companyAssets["AAPL"]=346000
    companyAssets["TSLA"]=82000
    PrintLn("Unsorted:")
    for k,v in pairs(companyAssets) do
        PrintLn(k .." " ..v)
    end
    PrintLn("Now Sorted:")
    local sortedKeys=getKeysSortedByValue(companyAssets,
                        function(a,b) return a<b end )
    for i,k in ipairs(sortedKeys) do
        PrintLn(k .." " .. companyAssets[k])
    end

end
```

Here is the output of this program:

```
Script output:
Unsorted:
MMM 46000
AAPL 346000
TSLA 82000
Now Sorted:
MMM 46000
TSLA 82000
AAPL 346000
```

As you can see the sorted list is printed in the order of increased asset amounts. The secret to this successfully sorted result is in that second "function" argument:

```
function(a,b) return a<b end
```

Notice that "<". It is called a comparison operator. It

143

compares a and b and returns "true" if a is less than b and false otherwise. The "function" argument defines an operation to compare members of the array. getKeysSortedByValue uses the "function" to sort members of the array based on the array member values (i.e., the total assets for the three companies specified in our script).

Let's have a look at the internals of the companyAssets array:

Those numbers are values and tickers are keys in the array. The "function" comparison "<" operator is applied to values only. getKeysSortedByValue returns a new array that looks like this internally:

The keys are now just ordered sequential numbers and the values in this array are keys from the input array to the getKeysSortedByValue command. This is in essence how sorting is done. It takes time to get used to how it works. It is not as simple as other commands in the system, but it is a very powerful command that can sort arrays using very complex conditions because the simple "<" less condition is just one possible way to define the comparison "function".

As you are familiar with sorting now, we can modify the dividends search algorithm. You can see the modified code on the next page, please take time and compare it to the original code:

And the printout looks like this:

```
AMOV 1.2691720784475 427.82  2.12 62154.06 181.93 -1.31
TKC 1.8258692555049 22.84  3.09 3937.88 189.31 -89.78
PDO 0.87054456321045 262.84  10.62 1562.69 0.00 0.15
DGICA 1.6829369249109 1.25  4.29 85.83 0.00 -82.24
BPT 0.84052673308131 197.89  30.86 242.25 0.00 0.00
VKI 1.1705463425332 52.90  4.55 404.09 72.47 -49.98
REFI 1.1739410175135 388.07  7.68 273.39 39.24 1.93
GPJA 2.0399374545104 21.44  5.05 226.44 142.14 -99.13
EMP 1.9194242708502 13.09  5.31 200.45 228.22 -95.69
BEDU 2.0272406521198 419.82  99.40 101.34 82.35 0.00
ETI-P 2.1097402462102 198.13  5.37 1163.59 213.96 -77.18
HCXY 2.0272070781244 6.66  6.19 3.27 112.08 -99.76
EAI 1.5379398393702 13.09  5.30 1083.83 228.22 -76.62
ENO 1.8859154929384 0.00  5.75 202.46 228.22 -95.80
Now Sorted:
ETI-P 2.1097402462102 198.13  5.37 1163.59 213.96 -77.18
GPJA 2.0399374545104 21.44  5.05 226.44 142.14 -99.13
BEDU 2.0272406521198 419.82  99.40 101.34 82.35 0.00
HCXY 2.0272070781244 6.66  6.19 3.27 112.08 -99.76
EMP 1.9194242708502 13.09  5.31 200.45 228.22 -95.69
ENO 1.8859154929384 0.00  5.75 202.46 228.22 -95.80
TKC 1.8258692555049 22.84  3.09 3937.88 189.31 -89.78
```

First you see the unsorted list of stocks (ticker,rank, yield, dividend, cap, debt-to-capital, and revenue growth), and then the sorted by rank list is presented in the print out.As you can see, sorting helps us see the highest-ranking companies first. In this case, ETI-P's rank is 2.1 which is the highest. Just for fun I looked at TKC with a rank of 1.8 and liked it more than the higher-ranking one. So always do manual research after getting scripting results. We will use sorting in the next chapter where we discuss how one can do the selling of portfolio positions.

```lua
local T=0
local unsorted={}
for T=0,GetTickerCount(),1 do
  local ticker=GetTickerByIndex(T)
  local today=GetTodayDay()
  local pastDay=today - 12*30
  local compRevenue=GetXBRL(ticker,today,"","mmRevenueTTM")
  local compRevenuePast=GetXBRL(ticker,pastDay,"","mmRevenueTTM")
  local divid=GetXBRL(ticker,today,"","mmDividendYield")
  local cap=GetXBRL(ticker,today,"","mmCapitalization")
  local debtToCap=GetXBRL(ticker,today,"","mmDebtToCapital")
  local stocksGrowth = GetXBRL(ticker,today,"","mmSharesOutstandingGrowthYoY")
  local percent = 100*(compRevenue - compRevenuePast)/compRevenuePast

  if  percent < 500 and percent >= 0 and compRevenuePast>0 and divid>0.5
    and debtToCap>=0  and debtToCap < 300 and cap>0 and stocksGrowth<5 then
      local percentRevenueSt=percent/100
      local dividSt=divid/50
      local capSt=cap/2000000
      local debtToCapSt = debtToCap/300
      local stocksGrowthSt = stocksGrowth/5
      local rank = 0.3*percentRevenueSt + 0.4*dividSt + 0.1*capSt
                     - 0.1*debtToCapSt - 0.1*stocksGrowthSt
      if rank > 0.8 then
          percent=string.format("%.2f",percent)
          divid=string.format("%.2f",divid)
          cap=string.format("%.2f",cap)
          debtToCap=string.format("%.2f",debtToCap)
          stocksGrowth=string.format("%.2f",stocksGrowth)

          PrintLn(ticker .. "  " .. rank.. " " ..percent .." " ..
              divid .. " " .. cap .. " " .. debtToCap .. " " .. stocksGrowth)

          local obj={}
          obj.ticker=ticker
          obj.rank=rank
          obj.percentYield=percent
          obj.cap=cap
          obj.divid=divid
          obj.debtToCap=debtToCap
          obj.stocksGrowth=stocksGrowth
          unsorted[ticker]=obj
      end
  end
end
PrintLn("Now Sorted:")
local sorted=getKeysSortedByValue(unsorted,
              function(a, b) return a.rank > b.rank end)

for _,key in ipairs(sorted) do
  local obj=unsorted[key]
  PrintLn(obj.ticker .. " " .. obj.rank.. " ".. obj.percentYield .." " ..
          obj.divid .. " " .. obj.cap .. " " ..
          obj.debtToCap .. " " .. obj.stocksGrowth)
end
```

19
ART OF SELLING

Warren Buffet famously said that he buys stocks with the intention to hold them forever. This might have been true, but if we analyze Berkshire Hathaway's quarterly reports, we can observe a lot of selling and re-balancing of their portfolio. Moreover, things change all the time and what used to be a good position yesterday might not be a good position today. It is also difficult to even define what a "good" position is. In this chapter, we will explore some strategies for selling. Please keep in mind that these are only my thoughts on the subject and they are not necessarily true. The purpose of this chapter is to show you how to build an algorithm which can help you identify stocks to sell which you can then modify for your own personal preferences.

Let's first define at least in vague terms what a good position is. Here is my definition: a good position is a position contributing to the overall diversification of the portfolio with a good balance of risk and reward. So each position should be considered for how much more value appreciation you expect from it versus the risks it bears, and how much income it can generate via dividends, and finally how well it contributes to overall portfolio's diversification. For positions that you held for a few years, the economic conditions could have changed completely and they might represent nothing of what they used to be. Why not sell them?

After trying various algorithms generating selling suggestions, I became a bit frustrated as the suggestions I was getting didn't make a lot of sense to me. Often the suggested positions that a human would clearly identify as "hold", the scripts identified as "sell". It is pretty hard to generate a reasonable sale suggestion. I would say harder than a stock buy suggestion! The reason why algorithms don't work so well on sale suggestions is due to a limited list of what you own. A typical DIY investor might have thirty or so positions overall. So you only have 30 variants to consider for selling. This pales in comparison to what you can buy. You always have thousands of possible stocks to choose from for purchase. So when a strategy for purchase is employed it traverses thousands of possibilities to pick the best matches. This simply doesn't work so well for selling where each of those 30 positions was uniquely picked using different strategies, then manually analyzed before finally making a purchase. So there was a lot of thought put into a purchase. Here is what I realized! You need to put down notes clearly detailing **why** you purchased a stock at the moment of purchase because over time you will forget the reason for the purchase. And if the reason for your purchase is no longer true, then it might be worth considering selling.

Let's say you decided to purchase a stock because it was growing fast and you found out that a lot of insiders recently bought it. Put a note down for that purchase transaction explaining this reasoning, ideally with the specific numbers (e.g. revenue growth of 20%, 3% of stocks bought by insiders recently). Then after 4 years have passed, if you look at these notes and check what happened to the stock price, (i.e., what happened to revenue growth, and if insiders were still buying it) then it would be a much easier decision. If the stock still stayed attractive at least relative to the reasons you had purchased it originally. I approach selling this way exactly.

Indeed the most common attributes I personally look for in stocks to buy are stock price in terms of how it changes overtime, and what shape the price curve has, revenue growth, and the debt levels of the company. Knowing that these are my 3 most important parameters for stock buying, I can develop a script that will analyze these 3 parameters as of the time I bought the stock, because I know I looked at those three to make a purchase decision. And then I check these three parameters at the time I am looking for candidates to sell.

```
local today=GetDayAsString(GetTodayDay());
PrintLn(today)
local arr={}
local arrRet={}
local arrRev={}
local arrDebt={}
CalcPortfolioStats("2020-01-01",today)
local positionCount=GetPositionCount()-1
for j=0,positionCount-1,1
do
  local ticker=GetPositionTicker(j)
  local remainQty=GetPositionValue(j,"EndPeriodTotalQty")
  if  remainQty > 0 then
    local totalReturn=GetPositionValue(j,"TotalReturnSinceBought")

    local boughtDay=GetPositionValue(j,"FirstBought")
    totalReturn=math.floor(totalReturn*(GetTodayDay()-boughtDay)/365)
    local revBought=GetXBRL(ticker,boughtDay,"","mmRevenue")
    local revNow=GetXBRLLatest(ticker,"","mmRevenue")
    local debtBought=GetXBRL(ticker,boughtDay,"","mmDebt")
    local debtNow=GetXBRLLatest(ticker,"","mmDebt")
    if revBought>0 and debtBought>0 and totalReturn>0 then
      local revPercent=math.floor( 100*(revNow-revBought)/revBought)
      local debtPercent=math.floor(100*(debtNow-debtBought)/debtBought)
      if revPercent~=0 and debtPercent  ~= 0 then
          if not(revPercent>1000 and debtPercent < 0) then
            local rank=totalReturn+3*debtPercent-3*revPercent
            arr[ticker]=rank
            arrRet[ticker]=totalReturn
            arrRev[ticker]=revPercent
            arrDebt[ticker]=debtPercent
            PrintLn(ticker .. ", return=" .. totalReturn ..
              ", debt=" .. debtPercent .. ", rev="..revPercent)
          end
      end
    end
  end --remain qty
end --for
--build table
local sortedKeys = getKeysSortedByValue(arr, function(a, b) return a > b end)
local tickers = "";
for _, key in ipairs(sortedKeys) do
  if tickers ~= "" then
    tickers = tickers .. ","
  end
  tickers = tickers .. key
end
local n=tablelength( sortedKeys)
DeleteTable("PortfolioSellReportPositives")
CreateTable("PortfolioSellReportPositives",4,n,
  "Rank,TotalReturn,RevenueChg,DebtChg",tickers,
  "Find candidates for selling among well performing positions");
local idx=0
for _, key in ipairs(sortedKeys) do
  SetTableValue("PortfolioSellReportPositives",0,idx,arr[key])
  SetTableValue("PortfolioSellReportPositives",1,idx,arrRet[key])
  SetTableValue("PortfolioSellReportPositives",2,idx,arrRev[key])
  SetTableValue("PortfolioSellReportPositives",3,idx,arrDebt[key])
  idx = idx + 1
end
```

I use sorting to order the candidates for selling based on how much revenue growth, debt, and price of the stock changed relative to the time the stock was purchased.

The generated table looks like this:

Script Tables	Custom Tables			✕

Table Name: PortfolioSellReportPositives

Name	Rank	TotalReturn	RevenueChg	DebtChg
TKC	327	21	43	145
CMI	211	10	21	88
CAT	54	24	34	44
LMT	48	30	26	32
AOS	35	14	7	14
MO	15	18	-10	-11
WM	-12	69	38	11
RTX	-22	11	15	4
CNI	-37	17	68	50
KHC	-62	13	-2	-27
DUK	-70	32	46	12

Let's look at the code step-by-step. We have 3 for-loops in total. The first for-loop iterates through the positions of the portfolio. For each position, the code determines the first purchase date by getting the "FirstBought" value. Then using that value we get the revenue, debt, and price at that moment in time. Then we also pull the current revenue, debt, and price. Having the old and the new values allows us to determine the change amounts percentage-wise. Then we calculate the rank of the stock in terms of how suitable it is for selling. So the higher the rank the more suitable it is for selling.

Let's look at the rank formula closer:

```
local rank=totalReturn+3*debtPercent-3*revPercent
```

TotalReturn contributes positively to the rank because of the line of thought here: "OK, we've got lucky and this stock has risen and we want to sell it now at this higher price to register our profits". This is a somewhat flawed line of thought as many investment experts would argue because if the stock appreciates in value that doesn't normally mean we should sell. I would agree with experts here except for one important condition: that high stock appreciation might not be justifiable anymore taking into account the other components of the rank formula. Let's look at them.

Debt growth contributes positively to the rank formula making the stock more desirable for a sale. Indeed the debt growth component works together with the stock appreciation component to boost the rank higher. If stock appreciated a lot and debt grew as well then the stock is a candidate for sale, if stock appreciated a little but debt grew a lot it also becomes desirable for selling.

Finally, revenue growth contributes negatively to the selling rank. Indeed if sales of the company are growing compared to when we bought it then we should probably hold on to this stock. So this component can neutralize the debt growth or the stock appreciation, but if the stock price grew **and** its debt grew then they both might overpower the revenue growth component and still make the stock a candidate for sale.

Now that we understand the core logic of the selling algorithm, we can look at the sorting logic just after the first for-loop:

```
local sortedKeys = getKeysSortedByValue(arr, function(a, b) return a > b end)
```

We already know that the resulting sortedKeys array will have tickers sorted from highest rank to lowest, because of the ">" sign in the "function" argument.

The next for-loop builds a comma-separated list of

tickers in the proper order which will be passed to the CreateTable command to form the row headers of the table. The final for-loop fills in the resulting table which we can see in the screenshot.

As you can see, the best positions for selling are not the ones that grew a lot in terms of price, but the ones that had an unfavorable combination of all three primary parameters. For example, the TKC sale suggestion is based on the fact that indeed we had some decent return on this position already of 21 percent, and we even had decent revenue growth, but the company took an enormous amount of debt more than doubling since my first purchase of this stock, so it became less attractive to keep it in the portfolio, especially for me personally since I don't like investing in high-debt businesses. On the contrary, another top candidate for selling is MO, which saw debt decrease by 11%, but it had its revenue growth negative so it scored pretty high as a business to sell. Knowing my investing style, I was probably initially attracted to MO because of its low debt and decent revenue growth. And now after it produced an 18% return, it might be a good candidate for selling since the revenue is falling and it is time to realize the 18% return and buy something else.

As you can see the algorithm is very unique to the individual investing style of each investor, and it is even unique to specific reasons for purchasing specific stocks. Moreover, the algorithm above is designed to find the candidates for sale among companies that already produced a decent return. So another natural approach to building a selling algorithm would be to pick the losers to sell. Not all stocks that dropped in price are "true losers" and should be sold to realize losses. In fact, if there is no numerical reason for a losing position to be sold it shouldn't normally be sold at all.

The algorithm above can be modified to search for the

highest ranking candidates for sale among losers. Let's first state what a good loser to sell can sound like: a company that lost money for me and I see no hope in its profit prospects, especially that which has also become higher risk with debt growth. So now let's adopt the rank formula to prioritize companies that sound like that:

```
local rank=-totalReturn+3*debtPercent-0.7*incomePercent-4*revPercent
```

As you can see the total return component has a minus in front. That is because we want to have a higher rank for companies that underperformed. We also have a new component: incomePercent. It also has a minus because if income is high we want to penalize the rank and push the company down the to-sell list.

Here is how the income component is calculated:

```
local incomeBought=GetXBRL(ticker,boughtDay,"","mmIncomeTTM")
local incomeNow=GetXBRLLatest(ticker,"","mmIncomeTTM")
local incomePercent=math.floor( 100*(incomeNow-incomeBought)/incomeBought)
```

Here is the output of this script:

Name	Rank	TotalReturn	RevenueChg	DebtChg	IncomeChg
GLT	479.7	-65	59	135	-351
TKC	225.2	21	43	145	24
BRFS	209.8	-70	-75	-80	-114
CMI	158.1	10	21	68	17
AMZN	57.9	-41	31	22	-107
MDT	48.4	-19	-3	3	-12
GLW	20.9	-15	-8	-15	-27
MO	7.9	18	-10	-11	-27

Table Name: PortfolioNegativesToSell

As you can see most of the top positions to sell are not the same as for the previous script that wanted to realize gains. This script has a different purpose: it wants to save you from

153

even more losses in your positions because the positions are "doomed". Look at GLT as a top pick. It has lost 65% of its value and on top of that, the position's debt has grown by 135% and income has decreased dramatically. I wouldn't sell this position despite all this though! I noticed a glimmer of hope in revenue growth. The revenue is not falling! This tells me that maybe the company is working hard to boost revenue with the hope to repair income in the future and that maybe they had to take on debt to either boost production or improve the supply lines. This is why you should never blindly follow algorithms, but investigate every company's unique situation in-depth. Interestingly, TKC is the next sale position in this algorithm, and it was one of the top picks in the positives for sale algorithm as well. Investing is an exciting and never-ending investigation! You see all these numbers and facts and you try to put the puzzle together and reconstruct what actually happened to the company, and honestly, the company's stock price plunge is to me the same as to Sherlock Holmes a crime scene to investigate. So reconstructing the crime scene in the stock market can be as exciting as solving real crimes!

Both of the above algorithms can be found on the Tickernomics web site in the public scripts section: PortfolioPositivesToSell and PortfolioNegativesToSell. These two algorithms show only one of millions of possible ways one can look at his/her portfolio and find the suggestions to sell. These algorithms do not consider many factors and probably the most important of those is how the portfolio diversification will be affected by a sale.

The next chapter will look at portfolio building from the diversification perspective.

20
PORTFOLIO BALANCING

In this chapter, we will develop a script to evaluate the effect of a stock purchase on the quality of our portfolio. This is only one of many ways the quality of a portfolio can be evaluated.

One of the most important measures of portfolio quality is diversification. There are many ways one can measure diversification, and I only demonstrate my approach, because it is easy to do and it is also easy to measure. I evaluate the diversification of a portfolio based on two parameters: sector and country. The more sectors your portfolio is comprised of, the more diversified it is. And the more countries your portfolio consists of, the more diversified it is.

For this approach, we will define the full diversification by country as to be 1 and no diversification to be 0. A full diversification is achieved when all countries are represented and they are represented equally. This is rarely needed in real life though. Then we can calculate the diversification of either of those by counting how many countries or sectors the portfolio is composed of and dividing by the total number of countries or sectors. For example, if the total number of countries available in the system is 100 and your portfolio has stocks from 5 countries that are all allocated in equal amounts then the diversification by country of the such portfolio is 5% (5*1/100 = 0.05).

When I said "allocated in equal amounts" I meant the stock's total value was equal across each country. This is rarely going to happen, so as usual to properly calculate the diversification we will have to use weighted position calculations. If out of those 5 countries, the value of US stocks is 1000 dollars and the other 4 countries' stocks are worth 100 dollars then of course the diversification will be pretty low:

1000*1/100 + 100*4/100)/1100 = 0.012. So only 1.2% diversification.

Let's develop a script to calculate both of those diversification measures, but first, we will print positions of the portfolio with their percentage of the total portfolio (weight), as well as country and sector:

```
local today=GetDayAsString(GetTodayDay());
CalcPortfolioStats("2020-01-01",today)
local positionCount=GetPositionCount()-1
for j=0,positionCount-1,1 do
  local ticker=GetPositionTicker(j)
  local remainQty=GetPositionValue(j,"EndPeriodTotalQty")
  if  remainQty > 0 then
    local percent=100*GetPositionValue(j,"PositionPercent")
    local sector=GetCompanyPropStr(ticker, "Sector")
    local country=GetCompanyPropStr(ticker, "Country")
    PrintLn(ticker .. " " .. string.format("%.2f", percent) ..
      "% ".. country .." " .. sector )
  end
end
```

CalcPortfolioStats calculates position returns and other parameters relative to the date specified as input. In this case, we chose a few years back and used the date January 1st, 2020 ("2020-01-01"). The printout looks like this:

DUK 1.49% United States Utilities
FMS 6.15% Germany Healthcare
FTS 1.35% Canada Utilities
GLT 1.19% United States Basic Materials
GLW 2.41% United States Technology
ICL 1.63% Israel Basic Materials
KHC 2.98% United States Consumer Defensive
KMB 2.72% United States Consumer Defensive

Armed with this knowledge, we can now build the actual diversification calculation. The reason why this preliminary printout is important is that we validated that the input data is correct and we can manually do a calculation with pen and paper to verify that the diversification algorithm produces valid results. When developing your own solutions, I highly recommend testing everything and printing as much detailed information as possible to catch mistakes because those mistakes can then cost a lot if investments are made based on wrong numbers.

Here is the diversification calculation code which is obviously based on the script we saw on the previous page:

```
local today=GetDayAsString(GetTodayDay());
CalcPortfolioStats("2020-01-01",today)
local positionCount=GetPositionCount()-1
local countryNum=61
local sectorNum=20
local countries={}
local sectors={}
for j=0,positionCount-1,1 do
  local ticker=GetPositionTicker(j)
  local remainQty=GetPositionValue(j,"EndPeriodTotalQty")
  if  remainQty > 0 then
    local percent=GetPositionValue(j,"PositionPercent")
    local sector=GetCompanyPropStr(ticker, "Sector")
    local country=GetCompanyPropStr(ticker, "Country")
    if sectors[sector]==nil then
      sectors[sector]=0
    end
    sectors[sector]=sectors[sector]+percent
    if countries[country]==nil then
      countries[country]=0
    end
    countries[country]=countries[country]+percent
  end
end -- end position for
local mySectorsNum=tablelength(sectors)
local myCountriesNum=tablelength(countries)
PrintLn(mySectorsNum .. "  " .. myCountriesNum)
local sectorDivers=0
for sector,percent in pairs(sectors) do
  sectorDivers=sectorDivers+percent*mySectorsNum/sectorNum
end
local countryDivers=0
for country,percent in pairs(countries) do
  countryDivers=countryDivers+percent*myCountriesNum/countryNum
end
PrintLn(math.ceil(100*sectorDivers) .. "%  " ..
        math.ceil(100*countryDivers) .."%" )
```

Here is the output:

2023-02-14 01:27:52: Script output:
2023-02-14 01:27:52: 9 8
2023-02-14 01:27:52: 45% 14%

As you can see the sector diversification looks pretty good at 45%, but the country diversification does not, as 14% seems like a low level of diversification in which my holdings are highly concentrated in one country.

These constants define how many sectors and countries are in the system:

```
local countryNum=61
local sectorNum=20
```

Notice that the "countries" and "sectors" arrays are used to collect the occurrences of unique countries and sectors within the portfolio. Then for-loops are used to calculate the weighted sum relative to the total possible diversification using all sectors and all countries equally:

```
local sectorDivers=0
for sector,percent in pairs(sectors) do
  sectorDivers=sectorDivers+percent*mySectorsNum/sectorNum
end
local countryDivers=0
for country,percent in pairs(countries) do
  countryDivers=countryDivers+percent*myCountriesNum/countryNum
end
```

We built a very useful diversification calculation algorithm in this chapter. I mentioned previously that another very important property of a portfolio is its total beta, which can also be calculated using a weighted summation method. Luckily we do not need to do that because we can pull portfolio beta with just one call:

```
GetPortfolioValue("TotalBeta")
```

As you know, the portfolio beta is also displayed on the portfolio page. Also, notice how diverse the industries are, hence we've got a 45% diversification score for economic sectors in the script:

So now equipped with the script from this chapter you can evaluate the impact that a purchase or a sale can have on your portfolio quality by entering a "test" transaction in the Transactions screen in Tickernomics.

The sequence of the evaluation can be as follows:

- ☐ Open the Portfolio screen and note the portfolio beta

- ☐ Run the script from this chapter and note the diversification scores (this script can be accessed in the Public Scripts library on Tickernomics by searching "AlgoInvestingChapter20")

- ☐ Open the Transactions screen

- ☐ Enter either a Sell or a Buy transaction depending on whether you are investigating the impact of a buy or a sell

- ☐ Open the Portfolio screen again and note the new beta for the portfolio

- ☐ Run the script again and note the new diversification scores.

- ☐ Compare before and after values of beta and diversification scores

- ☐ Make the decision whether the considered transaction is good for your portfolio. If it is not good then just delete the Transaction.

Of course, this is a long process, but remember that scripting is powerful enough to actually be able to generate transactions for you and delete the transactions later, so you could automate all these steps with your scripting. I will leave that for you to decide. In my case, I analyze the portfolio impact of the transaction only on the final stages of my decision process after I already did due diligence for a stock purchase or a stock sale, so I measure the portfolio impact as the final stage. I also enjoy looking at the visuals of the Portfolio screen to analyze the impact.

We learned how to do the diversification analysis in this chapter. We are moving quickly to the final pages of the core of this book. The next chapter will teach you some coding aspects that can help you a lot in your scripting. After that, we will get into various popular stock-picking techniques, which might be exciting for true geeks of the investment world!

21
DON'T DO TWICE

One of the main reasons why scripting is so good for investing tasks is that it allows you, the investor, to spend your time writing the script just once, and then you can reuse it over and over again to help with investments. This actually saves a lot of time in the long run, as well as prevents mistakes that humans so often do. Unfortunately, script writing itself is not an easy task and it can be a time-consuming task for more complicated scripts. At least there are techniques that can help shorten the time spent on script writing. We will learn some of them in this chapter.

In the previous chapter, we learned how to analyze the effects of buying and selling stocks on portfolio quality. There were a lot of steps to do that. What if we streamlined that process with a script? We already know how to add a transaction to a portfolio, but there is also a command to delete a transaction from a portfolio. So we can develop a script, which will display the portfolio quality before adding a transaction, then it will add a transaction and display the portfolio quality after adding that transaction, and finally, it will delete the transaction to return to the status quo. Wouldn't that be easier than what we did in the previous chapter? As a start, let's write a script to analyze a purchase transaction's effect on portfolio beta:

This is the script output and the script itself is on the next page:

```
2023-02-15 22:10:24: Script output:
2023-02-15 22:10:38: 0.76757465181562
2023-02-15 22:10:39: 0.78489755324379
```

The stock we purchased for this script is META. Notice the beta increased because META has a rather high beta, and in this demo we purchased a substantial number of META shares.

```
local today=GetDayAsString(GetTodayDay())
CalcPortfolioStats("2020-01-01",today)
local betaBefore=GetPortfolioValue("TotalBeta")
PrintLn(betaBefore)

SetTransactionValue(0,"TransactionType",1)
SetTransactionValueStr(0,"TransactionDate","2023-02-10")
SetTransactionValueStr(0,"Ticker","META")
SetTransactionValue(0,"Qty",30)
SetTransactionValue(0,"UnitPrice",200)
local trId=StoreTransaction(0)

CalcPortfolioStats("2020-01-01",today)
local betaAfter=GetPortfolioValue("TotalBeta")
PrintLn(betaAfter)

DeleteTransaction(trId)
```

As you can see, we first pull the TotalBeta value from the portfolio and print it, then we add a new META purchase transaction (30 shares at $200/share) and recalculate the portfolio. We pull the new TotalBeta and print it. Finally, we delete the inserted earlier transaction leaving the portfolio unchanged.

This is a very useful code if you want to ponder a purchase transaction for META stock, but let's modify this code so it would work for any stock. We will rewrite this code so it will take the input for the ticker name and quantity, as well as the type of transaction (1 for purchase and 2 for sale). We already used the input parameters feature in the Altman-Z score script. If you remember we had a ticker input parameter that the user could enter to calculate the Altman-Z score. We will modify the script above to have 3 parameters: ticker, quantity, and transaction type. We will pull the current stock price for the ticker so it won't be necessary to enter that manually. After all these changes, the script becomes useful for the purposes of estimating how portfolio beta will change if you try to execute the purchase or sale.

Here is the script:

```
--- Ticker, Qty, Enter 1 for purchase 2 for sale
function run(ticker, qty, transType)
    local today=GetDayAsString(GetTodayDay())
    CalcPortfolioStats("2020-01-01",today)
    local betaBefore=GetPortfolioValue("TotalBeta")

    SetTransactionValue(0,"TransactionType",transType)
    SetTransactionValueStr(0,"TransactionDate",today)
    SetTransactionValueStr(0,"Ticker",ticker)
    SetTransactionValue(0,"Qty",qty)
    local curPrice=GetXBRLLatest(ticker,"","mmStockPrice")
    SetTransactionValue(0,"UnitPrice",curPrice)
    local trId=StoreTransaction(0)

    CalcPortfolioStats("2020-01-01",today)
    local betaAfter=GetPortfolioValue("TotalBeta")
    PrintLn("Beta Before: " .. betaBefore..
            ", Beta After: " .. betaAfter  )

    DeleteTransaction(trId)
end
```

The result of running this script can be seen on the next page. Wouldn't it be nice if we somehow plugged the calculation for diversification of the portfolio that we did earlier into this script? It is a different script, so how can we reuse it in our current script? We could copy the diversification calculation code and paste it into the current script, but that would blow up the size of our current script, and also if we modified the diversification script it would not reflect in our current script. So what could we do? Luckily we can reuse scripts in other scripts with the use of the "require" command. This command takes the name of a script and automatically includes it in the current script where the command is used. Of course, this requires changes to the script because you cannot have a script with the same run() command.

The results from the previous script:

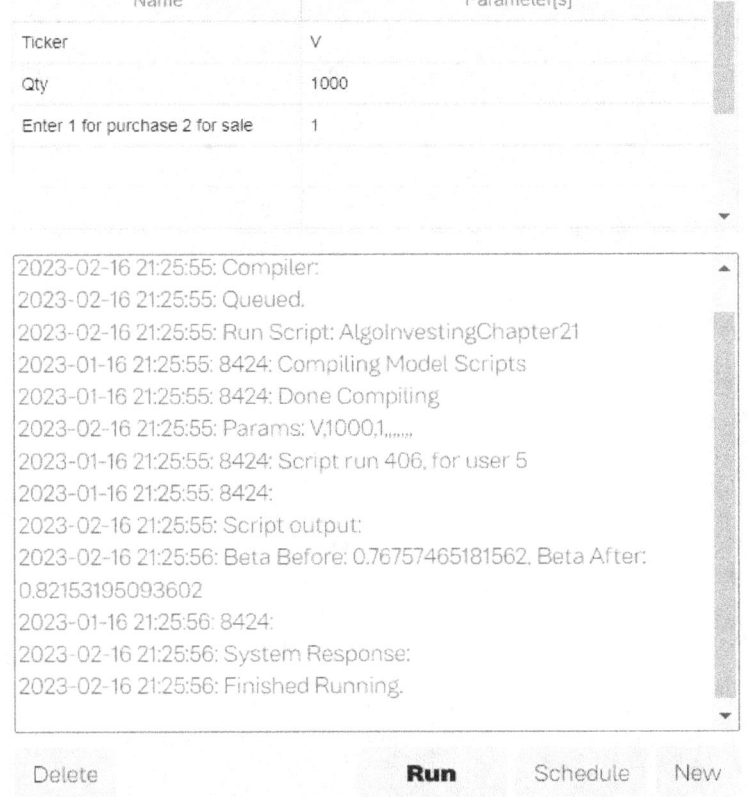

Name	Parameter[s]
Ticker	V
Qty	1000
Enter 1 for purchase 2 for sale	1

```
2023-02-16 21:25:55: Compiler:
2023-02-16 21:25:55: Queued.
2023-02-16 21:25:55: Run Script: AlgoInvestingChapter21
2023-01-16 21:25:55: 8424: Compiling Model Scripts
2023-01-16 21:25:55: 8424: Done Compiling
2023-02-16 21:25:55: Params: V,1000,1,,,,,,
2023-01-16 21:25:55: 8424: Script run 406, for user 5
2023-01-16 21:25:55: 8424:
2023-02-16 21:25:55: Script output:
2023-02-16 21:25:56: Beta Before: 0.76757465181562, Beta After:
0.82153195093602
2023-01-16 21:25:56: 8424:
2023-02-16 21:25:56: System Response:
2023-02-16 21:25:56: Finished Running.
```

Delete   **Run**   Schedule   New

So we should rename the run command in the
diversification script to printPortfolioDiversity like so:

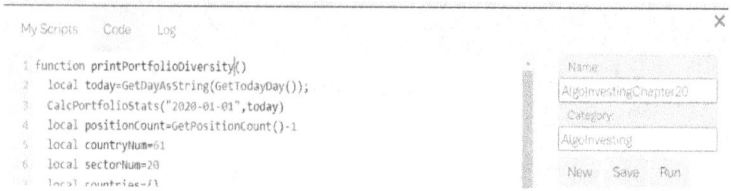

```
1 function printPortfolioDiversity()
2   local today=GetDayAsString(GetTodayDay());
3   CalcPortfolioStats("2020-01-01",today)
4   local positionCount=GetPositionCount()-1
5   local countryNum=61
6   local sectorNum=20
7   local countries={}
```

Name:
AlgoInvestingChapter20
Category:
AlgoInvesting
New   Save   Run

Then we can modify our stock transaction test script to reuse printPortfolioDiversity:

```
--- Ticker, Qty, Enter 1 for purchase 2 for sale
require "AlgoInvesting/AlgoInvestingChapter20"
function run(ticker, qty, transType)
    local today=GetDayAsString(GetTodayDay())
    CalcPortfolioStats("2020-01-01",today)
    local betaBefore=GetPortfolioValue("TotalBeta")

    printPortfolioDiversity()

    SetTransactionValue(0,"TransactionType",transType)
    SetTransactionValueStr(0,"TransactionDate",today)
    SetTransactionValueStr(0,"Ticker",ticker)
    SetTransactionValue(0,"Qty",qty)
    local curPrice=GetXBRLLatest(ticker,"","mmStockPrice")
    SetTransactionValue(0,"UnitPrice",curPrice)
    local trId=StoreTransaction(0)

    CalcPortfolioStats("2020-01-01",today)
    local betaAfter=GetPortfolioValue("TotalBeta")
    PrintLn("Beta Before: " .. betaBefore..
            ", Beta After: " .. betaAfter  )

    printPortfolioDiversity()

    DeleteTransaction(trId)
end
```

The "require" command is the key here as it allows you to include other scripts into your current script. This way you can also print diversification scores before and after the transaction.

We learned how to reuse code from different scripts so you wouldn't need to do a lot of copy-pasting. This opens Pandora's box in scripting as now you can create whole libraries of useful scripts to be reused by you or others. You can develop a complex system with many thousands of lines of code if necessary. You can go professional!

EVERYTHING MONEY 8 PILLARS

This chapter opens the series of chapters covering various popular techniques for picking stocks. They are described in this chapter and in the following few chapters. I personally do not use these techniques, but I have to cover them as many investors out there believe in these techniques and it is my duty to cover them, and also show how you can implement them in scripts. One thing I would advise about these techniques is that they are pretty popular and that means a lot of people use them, therefore their efficiency might have fallen since they were popularized. On the other hand, you can take any of these techniques as a starting point and build your personal approach on top of them. Moreover, it makes sense to combine these different techniques into one which might balance out the pros and cons of each individual technique. It is also interesting to learn the reasoning behind each of the techniques because learning the reasoning can teach us to ask the right questions about "why" certain parameters might work and others might not.

"Everything Money" is a popular YouTube channel that made a viral video about the "8 Pillars" investing technique. It is meant to be a "starting point" that investors can use to quickly understand a company's financial situation and valuation. Let's learn about this approach and the reasoning behind it. I will describe the technique first. The name of the technique implies there are 8 parameters to analyze when picking stocks. Here they are:

1. 5 Year average PE ratio
2. ROIC
3. 5-year revenue growth
4. 5-year net income growth

5. Shares outstanding change

6. LTL (long term liabilities) vs FCF

7. 5 year FCF growth

8. Price to FCF

PE is Price to Earnings and it is a very popular metric used by CNBC hosts and such to measure the price of companies because for some reason it is considered expensive when the Price of a company (also called capitalization) is above 20 times the earnings of a company. PE becomes negative if the company loses money. I like that 8 Pillars creators use 5-year averages because it protects us from sudden changes in a company's earnings in a specific quarter, such as a non-recurring loss or gain which can skew net income. The PE ratio is one of the parameters that is extremely sensitive to quarterly spikes. Earnings can change dramatically from quarter to quarter especially in specialized companies. Some companies are very seasonal and earnings are always bad for them in specific quarters. So PE ratio has to be analyzed as average over a longer period in my opinion, so I agree with 8 Pillars creators here.

ROIC stands for Return on Invested Capital. ROIC is calculated by dividing EBIT*(1- Tax Rate) by the average invested capital. Average Invested Capital is calculated in different ways, but the main point is the capital put into the company to generate earnings. So ROIC gives us this perception of how efficiently the invested capital is put to work. This is again a very subjective metric across different industries because everyone knows that there are capital-intensive industries such as pipelines or shipbuilding and then there are companies that don't use a lot of capital such as marketing agencies or IT consulting. So this metric only makes sense when it's used to evaluate companies within the same industry. Still, since we use 8 metrics combined we should get a well-balanced look into companies, so I am still fine with this technique. Let's move on to the next parameter.

Revenue Growth is something universal for all companies in all industries. I personally respect this parameter a lot and consider it probably the most important. The company's growth is measured by revenue growth. Revenue just has to grow year-over-year for a company to be considered attractive. However, even companies with declining or stagnant revenue can still make great investments at the right price. That being said, there are very few companies one can consider attractive that do not have revenue growing, and if a company is unable to grow revenue it risks being a victim to a hostile takeover at some point.

Profit growth sounds similar to Revenue Growth, but it is actually a completely different metric. Revenue Growth identifies if the company is growing, but Income Growth identifies if the company is healthy. A healthy company is not supposed to lose money or have its profits fall. If profits steadily decline you might pay attention as to why. Sometimes it can be a strategic decision by managers to trade profitability for growth in a company (for example drop prices in order to sell more, or invest in sales and marketing to garner more market share). So it is not always bad if profit growth is negative or stagnant. I think the 8 Pillars creators put Revenue Growth and Profit Growth together because they can move in opposite directions and can balance each other out in the formula.

The Shares Outstanding change metric is as important as the parameters used in the Dividend Source algorithm we developed in the previous chapters. It is important to make sure the company doesn't issue too many new shares diluting the existing shareholders. It is very common in REITs so watch out.

LTL stands for Long Term Liabilities. It is a standard category of liabilities in accounting and it includes things like long-term debts, contract obligations that last longer than a year such as lease liabilities, etc. FCF is Free Cash Flow. Probably doesn't need an introduction as it is the foundational parameter in Value Investing. FCF is a measure of the cash that is left for a company to spend on whatever it wants (dividends, share repurchases, acquisitions, debt paydowns) after everything that the business needs to run was subtracted from the cash received by the business. If you compare FCF to the average person's personal finances, then FCF is cash you have left at the end of the month after you spent money on food, bills, car repairs, etc. So what LTL to FCF ratio tries to measure is business solvency, because LTL is debt and FCF is free money, so if this ratio is too high then this person lives not according to their income by having too many debts relative to free cash they have left.

FCF itself is a parameter in the formula too just to make sure the business is cash flow positive.

Price-to-FCF is a metric similar to the PE metric, but why not have this one too?

So here we go: the 8 Pillars. Overall it all makes sense, but of course, the company is a much more complex organism and it would be naive to think that just these 8 metrics are enough. The good thing is we at least should get a list of decent companies to choose from. Now all that is left for this chapter is to give you the source code for this technique.

Quick note: The function used in the script below "GetValueForQuarterOffset" is designed to pull a value for a specific financial statement item for a specific quarter. To use this, the user enters the ticker, how many quarters back it would like to pull the data from (1 is the most recent quarter, 2 is 2 quarters ago, etc.), the segment (as previously mentioned, this is reserved for a future update to that site), and the XBRL tag name (e.g., "IncomeTaxExpenseBenefit" which is the tag name for

income tax expense you see at the bottom of an income
statement.

```lua
local arr = {} --Market cap
local arr1 = {} --5 year PE
local arr2 = {} --ROIC
local arr3 = {} --5 year revenue growth
local arr4 = {} --5 year net income growth
local arr5 = {}--shares outstanding change
local arr6 = {} --LTLvs5YearFCF
local arr7 = {} -- 5 year FCF growth
local arr8 = {} -- Price to FCF
local arr9 = {} -- Dividend yield
local arr10 = {} -- Dividend amount USD
local c=GetTickerCount()
local Labels=""

for i=0,c-1 do
  local ticker=GetTickerByIndex(i)

  --start of 8 pillar formula. Conditions:
  --1. 5 year Average PE under 22.5
  local MarketCap = GetXBRLLatest(ticker,"","mmCapitalization")
  local DividendYield = GetXBRLLatest(ticker,"","DividendYield")
  local DividendUSD = GetXBRLLatest(ticker,"","mmDividendUSD")
  local today = GetTodayDay()
  local LastYear = today - 365
  local TwoYearsAgo = today - (2*365)
  local ThreeYearsAgo = today - (3*365)
  local FourYearsAgo = today - (4*365)
  local CurrentIncome = GetXBRLLatest(ticker,"","mmIncomeAnnual")
  local LastYearIncome = GetXBRL(ticker,LastYear,"","mmIncomeAnnual")
  local TwoYearsIncome = GetXBRL(ticker,TwoYearsAgo,"","mmIncomeAnnual")
  local ThreeYearsIncome = GetXBRL(ticker,ThreeYearsAgo,"","mmIncomeAnnual")
  local FourYearsIncome = GetXBRL(ticker,FourYearsAgo,"","mmIncomeAnnual")
          FiveYearAverageIncome = (CurrentIncome+LastYearIncome+TwoYearsIncome
ThreeYearsIncome+FourYearsIncome)/5
FiveYearPE = MarketCap/FiveYearAverageIncome

  -- 2. ROIC
  local Goodwill = GetXBRLLatest(ticker,"","Goodwill")
  local Cash = GetXBRLLatest(ticker,"","CashAndCashEquivalentsAtCarryingValue")
  local Equity = GetXBRLLatest(ticker,"","mmBookValue")
  local Debt = GetXBRLLatest(ticker,"","mmDebt")
  local LongTermNotesPayable = GetXBRLLatest(ticker,"","LongTermNotesPayable")
  local NotesPayable = GetXBRLLatest(ticker,"","NotesPayable")
  InvestedCapitalCurrent = (Equity+Debt+LongTermNotesPayable+NotesPayable) -
          (Goodwill+Cash)
```

```
local today = GetTodayDay()
local PYear = today - 365
local PGoodwill = GetXBRL(ticker,PYear,"","Goodwill")
local PCash = GetXBRL(ticker,PYear,"","CashAndCashEquivalentsAtCarryingValue")
local PEquity = GetXBRL(ticker,PYear,"","mmBookValue")
local PDebt = GetXBRL(ticker,PYear,"","mmDebt")
local PLongTermNotesPayable = GetXBRL(ticker,PYear,"","LongTermNotesPayable")
local PNotesPayable = GetXBRL(ticker,PYear,"","NotesPayable")
InvestedCapitalPrior = (PEquity+PDebt+PLongTermNotesPayable+PNotesPayable) -
        (PGoodwill+PCash)

--define numerator variables

--operating profit past 12 months
local CurrentOperatingProfit = GetXBRLLatest(ticker,"","OperatingIncomeLoss")
local PQuarterOP1 = GetValueForQuarterOffset(ticker,2, "","OperatingIncomeLoss")
local PQuarterOP2 = GetValueForQuarterOffset(ticker,3, "","OperatingIncomeLoss")
local PQuarterOP3 = GetValueForQuarterOffset(ticker,4, "","OperatingIncomeLoss")
TotalOperatingProfit = CurrentOperatingProfit+PQuarterOP1+PQuarterOP2+PQuarterOP3

--Book taxes last 12 months
local CurrentBookTaxes = GetXBRLLatest(ticker,"","IncomeTaxExpenseBenefit")
local PQuarterTax1 = GetValueForQuarterOffset(ticker,2, "","IncomeTaxExpenseBenefit")
local PQuarterTax2 = GetValueForQuarterOffset(ticker,3, "","IncomeTaxExpenseBenefit")
local PQuarterTax3 = GetValueForQuarterOffset(ticker,4, "","IncomeTaxExpenseBenefit")
TotalIncomeTax = CurrentBookTaxes+PQuarterTax1+PQuarterTax2+PQuarterTax3

local CurrentDTL = GetXBRLLatest(ticker,"","DeferredIncomeTaxLiabilitiesNet")
local CurrentDTA = GetXBRLLatest(ticker,"","DeferredTaxAssetsNet")
local PriorDTA = GetXBRL(ticker,PYear,"","DeferredTaxAssetsNet")
local PriorDTL = GetXBRL(ticker,PYear,"","DeferredIncomeTaxLiabilitiesNet")
DTLChange = CurrentDTL-PriorDTL
DTAChange = CurrentDTA-PriorDTA
--Tax shield on interest
local CurrentIncomeBeforeTaxes = GetXBRLLatest(ticker,"",
    "IncomeLossFromContinuingOperationsBeforeIncomeTaxesExtraordinaryItemsNoncontrollingInterest")
local PQuarterIncomeBeforeTaxes1 = GetValueForQuarterOffset(ticker,2, "",
    "IncomeLossFromContinuingOperationsBeforeIncomeTaxesExtraordinaryItemsNoncontrollingInterest")
local PQuarterIncomeBeforeTaxes2 = GetValueForQuarterOffset(ticker,3, "",
    "IncomeLossFromContinuingOperationsBeforeIncomeTaxesExtraordinaryItemsNoncontrollingInterest")
local PQuarterIncomeBeforeTaxes3 = GetValueForQuarterOffset(ticker,4, "",
    "IncomeLossFromContinuingOperationsBeforeIncomeTaxesExtraordinaryItemsNoncontrollingInterest")
TotalIncomeBeforeTaxes = (CurrentIncomeBeforeTaxes+PQuarterIncomeBeforeTaxes1+
    PQuarterIncomeBeforeTaxes2+PQuarterIncomeBeforeTaxes3)

local CurrentInterestExpense = GetXBRLLatest(ticker,"","InterestExpense")
local PQuarterInterestExpense1 = GetValueForQuarterOffset(ticker,2, "","InterestExpense")
local PQuarterInterestExpense2 = GetValueForQuarterOffset(ticker,3, "","InterestExpense")
local PQuarterInterestExpense3 = GetValueForQuarterOffset(ticker,4, "","InterestExpense")
TotalInterestExpense = (CurrentInterestExpense+PQuarterInterestExpense1+PQuarterInterestExpense2+
    PQuarterInterestExpense3)
```

```
BookTaxRate = TotalIncomeTax/TotalIncomeBeforeTaxes
TaxShield = TotalInterestExpense*(BookTaxRate)
--Cash taxes paid
CashTaxes = TotalIncomeTax+(-DTLChange)+DTAChange+(-TaxShield)
--Return
RReturn = TotalOperatingProfit - CashTaxes

ROIC = (RReturn/(InvestedCapitalCurrent+InvestedCapitalPrior))*100

   --3. 5 Year revenue growth is positive (make this part of table)
   local CurrentRevenue = GetXBRLLatest(ticker,"","mmRevenueAnnual")
   local FiveYearsAgo = today - (5*365)
   local FiveRevenue = GetXBRL(ticker,FiveYearsAgo,"","mmRevenueAnnual")
   FiveYearRevenueGrowth = ((CurrentRevenue/FiveRevenue)^(1/5)-1)

   --4. 5 year net income growth is positive
   local CurrentIncome = GetXBRLLatest(ticker,"","mmIncomeAnnual")
   local FiveIncome = GetXBRL(ticker,FiveYearsAgo,"","mmIncomeAnnual")
   FiveYearIncomeGrowth = ((CurrentIncome/FiveIncome)^(1/5)-1)

  --5. Shares outstanding have decreased in the last 5 years
   local CurrentSharesOS = GetXBRLLatest(ticker,"","mmSharesOutstanding")
   local FiveSharesOS = GetXBRL(ticker,FiveYearsAgo,"","mmSharesOutstanding")
   FiveYearSharesOS = ((CurrentSharesOS/FiveSharesOS)^(1/5)-1)

  --6. Long term liabilities / 5 year avg FCF less than 5
   local CurrentFCF = GetXBRLLatest(ticker,"","mmFCFAnnual")
   local LastYearFCF = GetXBRL(ticker,LastYear,"","mmFCFAnnual")
   local TwoYearsFCF = GetXBRL(ticker,TwoYearsAgo,"","mmFCFAnnual")
   local ThreeYearsFCF = GetXBRL(ticker,ThreeYearsAgo,"","mmFCFAnnual")
   local FourYearsFCF = GetXBRL(ticker,FourYearsAgo,"","mmFCFAnnual")
   FiveYearAverageFCF=(CurrentFCF+LastYearFCF+TwoYearsFCF+ThreeYearsFCF+FourYearsFCF)/5
   local TotalLiabilities = GetXBRLLatest(ticker,"","Liabilities")
   local CurrentLiabilities = GetXBRLLatest(ticker,"","LiabilitiesCurrent")
   TotalLongTermLiabilities = TotalLiabilities-CurrentLiabilities
   LTLRatio = TotalLongTermLiabilities/FiveYearAverageFCF

  --7. 5 year growth in FCF (CFO-Capex)
   local FiveFCF = GetXBRL(ticker,FourYearsAgo,"","mmFCFAnnual")
   FiveYearFCFGrowth = ((CurrentFCF/FiveFCF)^(1/5)-1)

  --8. 5 year Price to FCF below 20
   FiveYearPriceFCF = MarketCap/FiveYearAverageFCF

--end of formula

   --if statements
   local Name=GetCompanyPropStr(ticker,"Name")
   local Sector=GetCompanyPropStr(ticker,"Sector")
   if not isNaN(FiveYearPE) and ROIC>9 and FiveYearPE<22.5 and FiveYearRevenueGrowth>0 and
     FiveYearIncomeGrowth>0 and FiveYearSharesOS<0 and LTLRatio<5 and FiveYearFCFGrowth>0 and
        FiveYearPriceFCF<20    and MarketCap>100 then
           arr[Sector.."/"..ticker]=MarketCap --{ticker,rank}
           arr1[Sector.."/"..ticker]=FiveYearPE --{ticker,rank}
           arr2[Sector.."/"..ticker]=ROIC --{ticker,rank}
           arr3[Sector.."/"..ticker]=FiveYearRevenueGrowth --{ticker,rank}
           arr4[Sector.."/"..ticker]=FiveYearIncomeGrowth --{ticker,rank}
           arr5[Sector.."/"..ticker]=FiveYearSharesOS --{ticker,rank}
           arr6[Sector.."/"..ticker]=LTLRatio --{ticker,rank}
           arr7[Sector.."/"..ticker]=FiveYearFCFGrowth --{ticker,rank}
           arr8[Sector.."/"..ticker]=FiveYearPriceFCF --{ticker,rank}
           arr9[Sector.."/"..ticker]=DividendYield --{ticker,rank}
           arr10[Sector.."/"..ticker]=DividendUSD --{ticker,rank}
      end --if statements
end --for i loop
```

```
local n=tablelength(arr)
DeleteTable("EverythingMoney8PillarStocks")
-- Println(tickers)
local i=0
for k, v in pairs(arr) do
  if Labels ~= "" then
    Labels = Labels .. ","
  end
  Labels=Labels..k
end
CreateTable("EverythingMoney8PillarStocks",11,n,
"MarketCap,FiveYearPE,ROIC,FiveYearRevenueGrowth,FiveYearIncomeGrowth,FiveYearShareChange,"..
"LTLvs5YearFCF,5YearFCFGrowth,Price/5YearFCF,DividendYield,DividendAmountUSD",Labels,"FiveYearPE");
for k, v in pairs(arr) do
  local temp1 = arr1[k]
  local temp2 = arr2[k]
  local temp3 = arr3[k]
  local temp4 = arr4[k]
  local temp5 = arr5[k]
  local temp6 = arr6[k]
  local temp7 = arr7[k]
  local temp8 = arr8[k]
  local temp9 = arr9[k]
  local temp10 = arr10[k]
  if not isNaN(v) then
    SetTableValue("EverythingMoney8PillarStocks",0,i,v)
    SetTableValue("EverythingMoney8PillarStocks",1,i,temp1)
    SetTableValue("EverythingMoney8PillarStocks",2,i,temp2)
    SetTableValue("EverythingMoney8PillarStocks",3,i,temp3)
    SetTableValue("EverythingMoney8PillarStocks",4,i,temp4)
    SetTableValue("EverythingMoney8PillarStocks",5,i,temp5)
    SetTableValue("EverythingMoney8PillarStocks",6,i,temp6)
    SetTableValue("EverythingMoney8PillarStocks",7,i,temp7)
    SetTableValue("EverythingMoney8PillarStocks",8,i,temp8)
    SetTableValue("EverythingMoney8PillarStocks",9,i,temp9)
    SetTableValue("EverythingMoney8PillarStocks",10,i,temp10)
    i=i+1
  end
end -- for k,v
StoreTable("EverythingMoney8PillarStocks")
Println("Done generating list - Go to Insight Tables and select EverythingMoney8PillarStocks from"..
" the drop down list to see the list of stocks")
```

Take your time to look through this script. It is a large chunk of code but you will learn a lot by taking the time and reading through it because if you understand it you can pretty much do code of any complexity. Even though this script is long, there is nothing new in this script that we didn't already do in the previous simpler scripts. It is simply longer because we analyze so many parameters. The most important part of the script is where we actually filter out the companies:

```
if not isNaN(FiveYearPE) and ROIC>9 and FiveYearPE<22.5 and FiveYearRevenueGrowth>0 and
FiveYearIncomeGrowth>0 and FiveYearSharesOS<0 and LTLRatio<5 and FiveYearFCFGrowth>0 and FiveYearPriceFCF<20
and MarketCap>100 then
```

This is the main condition and as you can see we make sure the PE is below 22.5 so the company is not overvalued. We make sure other parameters are positive or negative depending on what they are. We make sure the company's LTL ratio is below 5 so the company is not overly indebted. We make sure a company is big enough by checking market capitalization is above 100 million. We also check the price to FCF ratio is below 20.

Here is the result:

Items	MarketCap	PriceonPE	ROIC	FiveOneFlow	FivePivatence	FiveYearShare	LTLonYear/CF	SmallCFon	PricePilotFCF	GradualYield
Industrials/CHRW	12863.7855	18.2089	29.3008	0.1068	0.1326	-0.021	1.4451	0.1573	14.0825	2.2932
Basic Materials/UFPI	5298.2771	14.4149	19.4153	0.1961	0.4292	-0.0046	1.4296	0.0645	16.3836	1.1513
Industrials/ATKR	5232.1735	10.1315	27.5856	0.2108	0.5092	0.0488	1.9290	0.5586	14.1616	0
Basic Materials/LYB	31823.64	7.6691	10.4276	0.0601	0.0287	0.019	3.9776	0.301	7.6017	1.7676
Real Estate/WY	20771.8574	17.5082	9.069	0.0723	0.3497	-0.0064	2.3433	0.3456	12.463	2.2503
Financial Services/AX	3036.5364	16.0377	56.7509	0.1309	0.1231	-0.0142	3.4593	0.0646	12.2946	0
Basic Materials/NUE	42921.71	11.8051	23.8501	0.1246	0.3594	-0.0464	2.6296	0.2818	13.0338	1.1939
Healthcare/AMN	4075.6075	20.7589	13.9419	0.1491	0.1982	-0.0728	4.2807	0.0397	17.5363	0
Financial Services/FBP	2605.9854	12.6249	15.2446	0.1011	0.3923	-0.033	1.5065	0.0729	7.6174	3.2215

This was a long piece of code and not everyone will enjoy reading it. People can actually learn to like reading code. I myself never had patience reading someone else's code, but I learned to love it. Pick a calm time of the day when you are not in a rush. For me, it is usually the time just before I go to sleep. Brew some coffee or tea, or maybe even wine. Whatever works for you. Silence your phone. Print out the code above and take time to read it and try to understand what the person who wrote it meant to achieve. Just don't rush it. Try to enjoy it like reading a newspaper or a book. This is the way to enjoy reading code, at least that is what worked for me.

23

MAGIC FORMULA AND BUFFET

"The Little Book that Beats the Market" popularized the "Magic Formula" as the way to beat the market. It was written by a well-respected investor Joel Greenblatt. Greenblatt was the founder and former fund manager at Gotham Asset Management. He was also a graduate of the Wharton School at the University of Pennsylvania and an adjunct professor at Columbia University's business school. The book was a bestseller and of course, this formula was and is used by many people out there.

The main idea of the approach is to consider two main factors:

1. Return On Capital
2. Earnings Yield

Return on Capital is calculated as EBIT divided by a sum of Net Fixed Assets plus Working Capital. EBIT stands for Earnings Before Interest and Tax. Working Capital can be calculated as Current Assets minus Current Liabilities. Return On Capital is yet another popular metric of how efficiently capital is deployed to generate earnings.

Earnings Yield is calculated as EBIT divided by Enterprise Value. Enterprise value is the company's capitalization plus total debt minus cash of the company. Enterprise value sounds strange at first: why would you sum up capitalization and debt together and then subtract cash? What does the resulting amount stand for? Imagine you are a buyer of a company. You buy the whole company. You need to understand the true price you pay for the company. Capitalization is the total money you pay for the equity of the company, but the company might have debt, and you inherit this

177

debt when buying the whole company, so that is why you add the debt to capitalization, and you also subtract cash from the company because cash is a debt neutralizer. So Earnings Yield measures the true price of a company in relation to the company's earnings.

According to Greenblatt, how the actual trades are executed is also important. He meant to pre-select companies using the above two metrics and then purchase the top 30 or so at the beginning of the year. Then he also intended to sell the losing positions by the year's end to offset taxes with those losses and sell winners at the beginning of the year. Then each year the cycle should be repeated where an investor recreates the list, and invests in the new stocks that appear in it. It is important to note that some limitations to the size of companies and industries should be applied. It is only supposed to be used on larger companies and excludes REITs, financial companies, utility companies, non-US companies, etc.

I didn't try this approach so I cannot comment if it works. I do admit it seems to be "too simple" to work, but maybe it does! Anyways here is the code below for this approach:

```
local arr1 = {}
local arr2 = {}
local arr3 = {}
local arr4 = {}
local arr5 = {}
local arr6 = {}
local c=GetTickerCount()
local Labels=""
for i=0,c-1 do
  local ticker=GetTickerByIndex(i)
  --start of dividend stocks forumla
  local today = GetTodayDay()
  local FiveYearsAgo = today - (5*365)
  local FourYearsAgo = today - (4*365)
  local StockPriceFiveYearsAgo = GetXBRL(ticker,FiveYearsAgo,"","mmStockPrice")
  local StockPriceFourYearsAgo = GetXBRL(ticker,FourYearsAgo,"","mmStockPrice")
  local DividendsFiveYearsAgo = GetXBRL(ticker,FourYearsAgo,"","mmDividendUSD")
  ReturnFiveToFour = (((StockPriceFourYearsAgo-StockPriceFiveYearsAgo)+DividendsFiveYearsAgo)/
                      StockPriceFiveYearsAgo)*100
  local MarketCap = GetXBRLLatest(ticker,"","mmCapitalization")
  local CurrentEV = GetXBRLLatest(ticker,"","mmEV")
  --Operating income last 12 months
  local PQuarterOI0 = GetValueForQuarterOffset(ticker,1, "","OperatingIncomeLoss")
  local PQuarterFOI1 = GetValueForQuarterOffset(ticker,2, "","OperatingIncomeLoss")
  local PQuarterFOI2 = GetValueForQuarterOffset(ticker,3, "","OperatingIncomeLoss")
  local PQuarterFOI3 = GetValueForQuarterOffset(ticker,4, "","OperatingIncomeLoss")
```

```lua
local EBIT = PQuarterOI0+PQuarterFOI1+PQuarterFOI2+PQuarterFOI3
--fixed assets
local FixedAssets = GetXBRLLatest(ticker,"","PropertyPlantAndEquipmentNet")
--working capital
local CurrentAssets = GetXBRLLatest(ticker,"","AssetsCurrent")
local Cash = GetXBRLLatest(ticker,"","CashAndCashEquivalentsAtCarryingValue")
local ShortTermInvestments = GetXBRLLatest(ticker,"","ShortTermInvestment")
local AdjustedCurrentAssets = CurrentAssets-Cash-ShortTermInvestments
local CurrentLiabilities = GetXBRLLatest(ticker,"","LiabilitiesCurrent")
local IBLs = GetXBRLLatest(ticker,"","ShortTermBorrowingsAndCurrentPortionOfLongTermDebt")
local AdjustedCurrentLiabilities = CurrentLiabilities-IBLs
local WorkingCapital = AdjustedCurrentAssets-AdjustedCurrentLiabilities


local ReturnOnCapital=(EBIT/(FixedAssets+WorkingCapital))*100


local EarningsYield = (EBIT/CurrentEV)*100

--end of formula
local Name=GetCompanyPropStr(ticker,"Name")
local Industry=GetCompanyPropStr(ticker,"Industry")
local Sector=GetCompanyPropStr(ticker,"Sector")
local Country=GetCompanyPropStr(ticker,"Country")
if not isNaN(WorkingCapital) and not isNaN(ReturnFiveToFour) and Country=="United States" and
ReturnOnCapital<200 and EarningsYield<20.01 and MarketCap>100 and Sector~="Financial Services" and
Sector~="Utilities" and Industry~="REIT-Mortgage" and Industry~="REIT-Office" and
Industry~="REIT-Specialty"
and Industry~="REIT-Diversified" and Industry~="REIT-Hotel & Motel" and
   Industry~="REIT-Healthcare Facilities" and Industry~="REIT-Residential"
   and Industry~="REIT-Retail" and
   Industry~="REIT-Industrial"
   then
           arr1[Name.."/ "..Industry]=ReturnOnCapital --{ticker,rank}
           arr2[Name.."/ "..Industry]=EarningsYield --{ticker,rank}
           arr3[Name.."/ "..Industry]=CurrentEV --{ticker,rank}
           arr4[Name.."/ "..Industry]=MarketCap
           arr5[Name.."/ "..Industry]=ReturnOnCapital+EarningsYield
           arr6[Name.."/ "..Industry]=ReturnFiveToFour
   end
end --for i
local sortedKeys1 = getKeysSortedByValue(arr1, function(a, b) return a > b end)
local sortedKeys2 = getKeysSortedByValue(arr2, function(a, b) return a > b end)
local combinedArr={}
for index, key in ipairs(sortedKeys1) do
  combinedArr[key]=index
end
for index, key in ipairs(sortedKeys2) do
  combinedArr[key]=combinedArr[key] + index
end
local combinedArrSorted = getKeysSortedByValue(combinedArr, function(a, b) return a < b end)
```

```
DeleteTable("MagicFormulaInvesting")
-- PrintLn(tickers)
local i=0
for _, key in ipairs(combinedArrSorted) do
    if i < 20 then
        if Labels ~= "" then
          Labels = Labels .. ","
        end
        Labels=Labels..key
    end
end -- for k,v

CreateTable("MagicFormulaInvesting",5,20,
"ReturnOnCapital,EarningsYield,EnterpriseValue,MarketCap,Rank",
    Labels,"ReturnOnCapital");
i=0
for _, k in ipairs(combinedArrSorted) do
    if i < 20 then
      PrintLn(k)
        local temp1 = arr1[k]
        local temp2 = arr2[k]
        local temp3 = arr3[k]
        local temp4 = arr4[k]
        local temp6 = arr6[k]
        if not isNaN(temp1) then
          SetTableValue("MagicFormulaInvesting",0,i,temp1)
          SetTableValue("MagicFormulaInvesting",1,i,temp2)
          SetTableValue("MagicFormulaInvesting",2,i,temp3)
          SetTableValue("MagicFormulaInvesting",3,i,temp4)
          SetTableValue("MagicFormulaInvesting",4,i,i+1)
          --SetTableValue("MagicFormulaInvesting",5,i,temp6)
          i=i+1
        end
    end
end -- for k,v
StoreTable("MagicFormulaInvesting")
PrintLn("Done finding Stocks - Go to Insight Tables and select MagicFormulaInvesting from the drop "..
"down list to see the list of stocks")
```

As a bonus, let me also give you Warren Buffet's Owner's Earnings algorithm in this chapter. It is a very popular investment approach popularized by probably the most famous investor of all - Mr. Warren Buffet. I give it in this chapter because to me it is kind of similar to the approach above.

There is some controversy about how exactly Owners' Earnings should be calculated so I will give the exact Buffet's definition:
"These represent (a) reported earnings plus (b) depreciation, depletion, amortization, and certain other non-cash charges ... less (c) the average annual amount of capitalized expenditures

for plant and equipment, etc. that the business requires to fully maintain its long-term competitive position and its unit volume ... Our owner-earnings equation does not yield the deceptively precise figures provided by GAAP, since (c) must be a guess - and one sometimes very difficult to make. Despite this problem, we consider the owner earnings figure, not the GAAP figure, to be the relevant item for valuation purposes ... All of this points to the absurdity of the 'cash flow' numbers that are often set forth in Wall Street reports. These numbers routinely include (a) plus (b) - but do not subtract (c)."

We will calculate Owners' Earnings as Operating Cash Flow (OCF) minus Maintenance Capital Expenditure (MCE). OCF is reported on a companies' statement of cash flows and measures the money produced by, or used in, normal company operations such as selling goods and services, processing orders, etc. MCE is simply CapEx minus Growth CapEx. CapEx is short for capital expenditures and is funds used by a company to acquire, upgrade, and maintain physical assets such as property, plants, buildings, technology, or equipment. Growth CapEx is a form of capital expenditure undertaken by a company to expand existing operations or further growth prospects. It can be difficult to determine exactly how much of a company's CapEx is growth CapEx or maintenance CapEx. Sometimes a company will explicitly state how much each one is, but most of the time we will have to estimate what it is. For this script, we use a method popularized by Bruce Greenwald, a former professor at Columbia University, to estimate growth CapEx. This formula calculates the gross PPE (property, plant, and equipment) balance as a % of revenue, averaged for the past 5 years - the gross PPE/Revenue Ratio, then calculates the percentage change in gross PPE over a given period of time (i.e., one quarter, one year) and then multiples the gross PPE/Sales ratio to the percentage change in gross PPE (which is the same thing as CapEx) to determine approximately how much CapEx was required to "support" the revenue growth over that period. The rest of the CapEx is assumed to be maintenance CapEx. So

Owner's Earnings signifies the "true earnings" of the business since they exclude CapEx that is intended to expand the business as opposed to the CapEx that is required to maintain the current level of operations. In a way, growth CapEx is similar to a business acquisition in that its purpose is to expand the size of the business? Yes, there are many ways one can measure "true earnings" and this is Buffett's preferred way.

The way one picks stocks using Owners' Earnings is to find the lowest ratios of capitalization to Owners' Earnings because it is supposed to be a superior measure compared to the PE ratio, which doesn't account for maintenance/growth CapEx and such. This is an open discussion of course and since I do not use this approach either I will not argue whether it is better or not. I will provide code to calculate it though:

```
function run(ticker)

--Formula is Operating Cash Flow less maintenance capital expenditures

    local CurrentQuarterOCF = GetXBRLLatest(ticker,"","NetCashProvidedByUsedInOperatingActivities")
    local CurrentCapex = GetXBRLLatest(ticker,"","PaymentsToAcquirePropertyPlantAndEquipment")
    local Revenue = GetXBRLLatest(ticker,"","mmRevenueAnnual")
    local PPE = GetXBRLLatest(ticker,"","PropertyPlantAndEquipmentGross")
    local MCap = GetXBRLLatest(ticker,"","mmCapitalization")
    local PE = GetXBRLLatest(ticker,"","mmPE")

     --Need to get prior year mmRevenue and PPE going back 5 years, must be dynamic based past year
    local today = GetTodayDay()
    local PYear = today - 365
    local PYRevenue = GetXBRL(ticker,PYear,"","mmRevenueAnnual")
    local PYPPE = GetXBRL(ticker,PYear,"","PropertyPlantAndEquipmentGross")

    --2 years ago
    local TwoYearsAgo = today - (365*2)
    local TwoYearsAgoRevenue = GetXBRL(ticker,TwoYearsAgo,"","mmRevenueAnnual")
    local TwoYearsAgoPPE = GetXBRL(ticker,TwoYearsAgo,"","PropertyPlantAndEquipmentGross")
```

```
--3 years ago
local ThreeYearsAgo = today - (365*3)
local ThreeYearsAgoRevenue = GetXBRL(ticker,ThreeYearsAgo,"","mmRevenueAnnual")
local ThreeYearsAgoPPE = GetXBRL(ticker,ThreeYearsAgo,"","PropertyPlantAndEquipmentGross")

--4 years ago
local FourYearsAgo = today - (365*4)
local FourYearsAgoRevenue = GetXBRL(ticker,FourYearsAgo,"","mmRevenueAnnual")
local FourYearsAgoPPE = GetXBRL(ticker,FourYearsAgo,"","PropertyPlantAndEquipmentGross")

--5 years ago
local FiveYearsAgo = today - (365*5)
local FiveYearsAgoRevenue = GetXBRL(ticker,FiveYearsAgo,"","mmRevenueAnnual")
local FiveYearsAgoPPE = GetXBRL(ticker,FiveYearsAgo,"","PropertyPlantAndEquipmentGross")


--GrossPPE to Revenue Ratio for past 5 years
local PPERevenueRatio = (PYPPE+TwoYearsAgoPPE+ThreeYearsAgoPPE+FourYearsAgoPPE+FiveYearsAgoPPE)
    /(PYRevenue+TwoYearsAgoRevenue+ThreeYearsAgoPPE+FourYearsAgoRevenue+FiveYearsAgoRevenue)


--Get OCF for 3 past quarters
--GetValueForQuarterOffset(ticker,2,"","InterestExpenseDebt")
local PQuarterOCF1 = GetValueForQuarterOffset(ticker,2,"","NetCashProvidedByUsedInOperatingActivities")
local PQuarterOCF2 = GetValueForQuarterOffset(ticker,3,"","NetCashProvidedByUsedInOperatingActivities")
local PQuarterOCF3 = GetValueForQuarterOffset(ticker,4,"","NetCashProvidedByUsedInOperatingActivities")
--Get Capex for past 3 quarters
local PQuarterCapex1 = GetValueForQuarterOffset(ticker,2,"","PaymentsToAcquirePropertyPlantAndEquipment")
local PQuarterCapex2 = GetValueForQuarterOffset(ticker,3,"","","PaymentsToAcquirePropertyPlantAndEquipmen
local PQuarterCapex3 = GetValueForQuarterOffset(ticker,4,"","PaymentsToAcquirePropertyPlantAndEquipment")

--Calculate maintenance capex
local TotalCapex = CurrentCapex + PQuarterCapex1 + PQuarterCapex2 + PQuarterCapex3
local GrowthCapex = ((PPE-PYPPE)*PPERevenueRatio)
local MaintCapex = TotalCapex - GrowthCapex

-- Define outputs

local OE = ((CurrentQuarterOCF + PQuarterOCF1 + PQuarterOCF2 + PQuarterOCF3) - MaintCapex)
local PriceToOwnersEarnings = MCap/(OE)

--Maintenance capital expenditures calculated using Bruce Greenwald formula from his book:
--Value Investing: From Graham to Buffett and Beyond,

PrintLn("Owners' Earnings = Operating Cash Flow ("..(CurrentQuarterOCF + PQuarterOCF1 + PQuarterOCF2
    + PQuarterOCF3).."") less maintenance capital expenditures ("..MaintCapex..").")
PrintLn("Owners' Earnings for this stock in the past year was "..OE)
PrintLn("The Price/Owners Earnings ratio is "..PriceToOwnersEarnings)
PrintLn("The Price/Earnings ratio is "..PE)
```

The next chapter will be the last chapter looking at various popular investing techniques. We could continue forever since there are so many different ways to invest and we should stop at some point. Also, a lot of techniques start to resemble one another so our purpose here is to teach the patterns so you can take over and develop your own unique ways.

24
FRENCH AND MORE

Eugene Fama and Kenneth French introduced the three-factor model in 1993. The idea was to add two more factors to the capital asset pricing model (CAPM): small minus big (SMB), which represents the return spread between small- and large-cap stocks, and high minus low (HML), which measures the return spread between high book-to-cap and low book-to-cap stocks.

The CAPM, if you remember, uses the beta of a stock to measure its out-performance and under-performance relative to the market, but CAPM didn't account for the specifics of a company's typical return behavior, and finance researchers noticed that some stocks were generating returns that were unexplained by beta only. Beta is too generic and it doesn't account for example for the size of the company. So it is logical to add the SMB factor to account for the difference in returns between a large and a small company. The same logic applies to HML which accounts for the return difference between "value" stocks (usually high book value) and growth stocks (usually low book value).

Later on, two more factors were added to the three factor model. RMW is the return spread of the most profitable firms vs the least profitable (it stands for "robust minus weak", meaning companies with robust versus weak operating profitability. CMA is the return spread of firms that invest back into themselves conservatively vs aggressively, and it posits that companies with more conservative reinvestment policies tend to have higher expected returns than companies with more aggressive reinvestment policies. Do you see the pattern? You actually could add even more factors beyond five if you wanted to. There is currently no proof that more factors would better explain asset pricing as there have been plenty of research published attempting to explain a new factor, but oftentimes a new factor is just an already existing factor masking as something else. The five factor model is the most well-regarded model at present time.

Here is how the formula progression looks like. First we just have CAPM with alpha, beta and difference between the market return and risk free return, commonly referred to as the "market risk premium":

$$\textbf{CAPM} = a_i + b_i(R_{Mt} - R_{Ft})$$

Then 3 factor Fama French:

$$R = a_i + b_i(R_{Mt} - R_{Ft}) + s_i SMB_t + h_i HML_t$$

Then 5 factor Fama French:

$$R = a_i + b_i(R_{Mt} - R_{Ft}) + s_i SMB_t + h_i HML_t + r_i RMW_t + c_i CMA_t$$

Then we can add in similar fashion more factors if we want to.

It is time to give you the code which will filter out companies fitting the 5 factor Fama French model. It is important to note that the 5 factor model is not a stock picking strategy, but a portfolio construction strategy. The whole purpose of the script below is to generate a list of stocks that have qualities similar to what the Fama-French model states would lead to high expected returns, so that we can research them further.

```lua
--Need to filter out financial services and REITs
--The five factors are: Size (small caps tend to be better - 500M to 3B),
--value (low P/B are better - below 2.25x)
--profitability (higher operating profitability is better - current operating margin above 12.5%
--and 5 year average above 10%)
--investment (conservative investment is better than aggressive - Book value must be lower than
--5x what it was 5 years ago)
-- And beta must be at least 1

function run()
    local arr = {}
    local arr1 = {}
    local arr2 = {}
    local arr3 = {}
    local arr4 = {}
    local arr5 = {}
    local arr6 = {}
    local c=GetTickerCount()
    local Labels=""
  for i=0,c-1 do
   local ticker=GetTickerByIndex(i)

    --start of formula
    local MarketCap = GetXBRLLatest(ticker,"","mmCapitalization")
    local CurrentBookValue = GetXBRLLatest(ticker,"","mmBookValue")
    CurrentPB = MarketCap/CurrentBookValue

    --dividend yield
    local DividendYield = GetXBRLLatest(ticker,"","mmDividendYield")

    local today = GetTodayDay()
    local FiveYearsAgo = today - (5*365)

    local BookValueFiveYearsAgo = GetXBRL(ticker,FiveYearsAgo,"","mmBookValue")
    PBRatio = CurrentBookValue/BookValueFiveYearsAgo
    FiveYearBookValueGrowth = (((CurrentBookValue/BookValueFiveYearsAgo)^(1/5))-1)*100

    --Beta of at least 1
    local Beta = GetXBRLLatest(ticker,"","mmBeta")

    --Robust operating profitability
      --Operating income
    local CurrentOM = GetXBRLLatest(ticker,"","OperatingIncomeLoss")
    local PQuarterOM1 = GetValueForQuarterOffset(ticker,2, "","OperatingIncomeLoss")
    local PQuarterOM2 = GetValueForQuarterOffset(ticker,3, "","OperatingIncomeLoss")
    local PQuarterOM3 = GetValueForQuarterOffset(ticker,4, "","OperatingIncomeLoss")
    TTMOM = CurrentOM+PQuarterOM1+PQuarterOM2+PQuarterOM3

    local CurrentRevenue = GetXBRLLatest(ticker,"","mmRevenue")
    local PQuarterRev1 = GetValueForQuarterOffset(ticker,2, "","mmRevenue")
    local PQuarterRev2 = GetValueForQuarterOffset(ticker,3, "","mmRevenue")
    local PQuarterRev3 = GetValueForQuarterOffset(ticker,4, "","mmRevenue")
    TTMRevenue = CurrentRevenue+PQuarterRev1+PQuarterRev2+PQuarterRev3

    CurrentOperatingMargin = (TTMOM/TTMRevenue)*100
```

```lua
local PQuarterOM4 = GetValueForQuarterOffset(ticker,5, "","OperatingIncomeLoss")
local PQuarterOM5 = GetValueForQuarterOffset(ticker,6, "","OperatingIncomeLoss")
local PQuarterOM6 = GetValueForQuarterOffset(ticker,7, "","OperatingIncomeLoss")
local PQuarterOM7 = GetValueForQuarterOffset(ticker,8, "","OperatingIncomeLoss")

local PQuarterOM8 = GetValueForQuarterOffset(ticker,9, "","OperatingIncomeLoss")
local PQuarterOM9 = GetValueForQuarterOffset(ticker,10, "","OperatingIncomeLoss")
local PQuarterOM10 = GetValueForQuarterOffset(ticker,11, "","OperatingIncomeLoss")
local PQuarterOM11 = GetValueForQuarterOffset(ticker,12, "","OperatingIncomeLoss")

local PQuarterOM12 = GetValueForQuarterOffset(ticker,13, "","OperatingIncomeLoss")
local PQuarterOM13 = GetValueForQuarterOffset(ticker,14, "","OperatingIncomeLoss")
local PQuarterOM14 = GetValueForQuarterOffset(ticker,15, "","OperatingIncomeLoss")
local PQuarterOM15 = GetValueForQuarterOffset(ticker,16, "","OperatingIncomeLoss")

local PQuarterOM16 = GetValueForQuarterOffset(ticker,17, "","OperatingIncomeLoss")
local PQuarterOM17 = GetValueForQuarterOffset(ticker,18, "","OperatingIncomeLoss")
local PQuarterOM18 = GetValueForQuarterOffset(ticker,19, "","OperatingIncomeLoss")
local PQuarterOM19 = GetValueForQuarterOffset(ticker,20, "","OperatingIncomeLoss")
TotalFiveYearOM = TTMOM+PQuarterOM4+PQuarterOM5+PQuarterOM6+PQuarterOM7+PQuarterOM8+
PQuarterOM9+PQuarterOM10+PQuarterOM11+PQuarterOM12+PQuarterOM13+PQuarterOM14+PQuarterOM15
+PQuarterOM16+PQuarterOM17+PQuarterOM18+PQuarterOM19
    --Revenue
local PQuarterRevenue4 = GetValueForQuarterOffset(ticker,5, "","mmRevenue")
local PQuarterRevenue5 = GetValueForQuarterOffset(ticker,6, "","mmRevenue")
local PQuarterRevenue6 = GetValueForQuarterOffset(ticker,7, "","mmRevenue")
local PQuarterRevenue7 = GetValueForQuarterOffset(ticker,8, "","mmRevenue")

local PQuarterRevenue8 = GetValueForQuarterOffset(ticker,9, "","mmRevenue")
local PQuarterRevenue9 = GetValueForQuarterOffset(ticker,10, "","mmRevenue")
local PQuarterRevenue10 = GetValueForQuarterOffset(ticker,11, "","mmRevenue")
local PQuarterRevenue11 = GetValueForQuarterOffset(ticker,12, "","mmRevenue")

local PQuarterRevenue12 = GetValueForQuarterOffset(ticker,13, "","mmRevenue")
local PQuarterRevenue13 = GetValueForQuarterOffset(ticker,14, "","mmRevenue")
local PQuarterRevenue14 = GetValueForQuarterOffset(ticker,15, "","mmRevenue")
local PQuarterRevenue15 = GetValueForQuarterOffset(ticker,16, "","mmRevenue")

local PQuarterRevenue16 = GetValueForQuarterOffset(ticker,17, "","mmRevenue")
local PQuarterRevenue17 = GetValueForQuarterOffset(ticker,18, "","mmRevenue")
local PQuarterRevenue18 = GetValueForQuarterOffset(ticker,19, "","mmRevenue")
local PQuarterRevenue19 = GetValueForQuarterOffset(ticker,20, "","mmRevenue")
TotalFiveYearRevenue = TTMRevenue+PQuarterRevenue4+PQuarterRevenue5+PQuarterRevenue6+
    PQuarterRevenue7+PQuarterRevenue8+PQuarterRevenue9+PQuarterRevenue10+PQuarterRevenue11+
    PQuarterRevenue12+PQuarterRevenue13+PQuarterRevenue14+PQuarterRevenue15+PQuarterRevenue16+
    PQuarterRevenue17+PQuarterRevenue18+PQuarterRevenue19

FiveYearAverageOperatingMargin = (TotalFiveYearOM/TotalFiveYearRevenue)*100
    --end of formula
    --if statements
    local Name=GetCompanyPropStr(ticker,"Name")
    local Industry=GetCompanyPropStr(ticker,"Industry")
    local Sector=GetCompanyPropStr(ticker,"Sector")
    if not isNaN(FiveYearBookValueGrowth) and CurrentPB<2.25 and CurrentPB>0 and
MarketCap>500 and MarketCap<2500 and PBRatio<7.5 and CurrentOperatingMargin>12.5 and
FiveYearAverageOperatingMargin>10 and Beta>1 then

        arr[Name.."/ "..Industry]=MarketCap --(ticker,rank)
        arr1[Name.."/ "..Industry]=CurrentPB --(ticker,rank)
        arr2[Name.."/ "..Industry]=CurrentOperatingMargin --(ticker,rank)
        arr3[Name.."/ "..Industry]=FiveYearAverageOperatingMargin --(ticker,rank)
        arr4[Name.."/ "..Industry]=Beta --(ticker,rank)
```

188

```
        arr5[Name.."/ "..Industry]=FiveYearBookValueGrowth --{ticker,rank}
        arr6[Name.."/ "..Industry]=DividendYield --{ticker,rank}
        end --if statements
end --for i
   local n=tablelength(arr)
   DeleteTable("FamaFrenchFactorModelStocks")
   -- PrintLn(tickers)
   local i=0
   for k, v in pairs(arr) do
      if Labels ~= "" then
      Labels = Labels .. ","
    end
       Labels=Labels..k
       end
   CreateTable("FamaFrenchFactorModelStocks",7,n,"MarketCap,Price/BookRatio,CurrentOperatingMargin,"..
    "FiveYearAverageOperatingMargin,Beta,FiveYearBookValueGrowth,DividendYield",Labels,
    "FamaFrenchFactorModelStocks");
      for k, v in pairs(arr) do
         local temp1 = arr1[k]
         local temp2 = arr2[k]
         local temp3 = arr3[k]
         local temp4 = arr4[k]
         local temp5 = arr5[k]
         local temp6 = arr6[k]
         if not isNaN(v) then
            SetTableValue("FamaFrenchFactorModelStocks",0,i,v)
            SetTableValue("FamaFrenchFactorModelStocks",1,i,temp1)
            SetTableValue("FamaFrenchFactorModelStocks",2,i,temp2)
            SetTableValue("FamaFrenchFactorModelStocks",3,i,temp3)
            SetTableValue("FamaFrenchFactorModelStocks",4,i,temp4)
            SetTableValue("FamaFrenchFactorModelStocks",5,i,temp5)
            SetTableValue("FamaFrenchFactorModelStocks",6,i,temp6)
            i=i+1
         end
      end -- for k,v
   StoreTable("FamaFrenchFactorModelStocks")
PrintLn("Done generating list - Go to Insight Tables and select FamaFrenchFactorModelStocks from the"..
 " drop down list to see the list of stocks")
```

Another interesting approach to analyzing stocks based on various metrics was devised by Joseph Piotroski, a Stanford accounting professor, and was later popularized by SmartMoney magazine and Bloomberg BusinessWeek. Unlike other methods that rank companies based on a formula that uses standard mathematical operations to get the numeric score, Piotroski uses a fixed score from zero to nine, where nine is the desirable highest score. Piotroski's score tries to balance profitability parameters, operating efficiency parameters, leverage, liquidity, and the number of shares issued. Each of those parameters adds or doesn't add 1 to the total score. The "best" company will get 1 for each of the parameters. Here is the full list of nine parameters, each awarding one point to the total Piotroski score:

1. Gross Profit margin for the current year is higher than the previous year
2. Positive Net Income for the year
3. Return On Assets above zero (earnings to assets ratio)
4. OCF is positive for the year (or FCF, OCF stands for operating cash flow)
5. Long Term Debt decreased this year
6. The current Assets to Current Liabilities ratio improved this year
7. No Share Dilution during the current year
8. Assets Turnover improved this year. Assets Turnover is calculated as annual revenue divided by the average total assets
9. OCF is higher than the income

The one problem with this score a person can immediately notice is that it is an all-or-nothing score. For example, if net income is just slightly below zero then the company will not get the point versus the company that has income just slightly above zero. The same applies to all points. There are versions of the Piotroski score that use the fractional scoring technique. Moreover, because there are so many metrics, and some of them kind of overlap with what they try to measure, the overall score is quite objective. I will give you the code to do an all-or-nothing Piotroski version of the algorithm:

```
---Enter ticker here -->

function run(ticker)

    local today = GetTodayDay()
    local PYear = today - 365
    local TwoYears = today - (2*365)

    local CurrentGPM=GetXBRLLatest(ticker,"","mmGrossProfitMargin")
    local PriorGPM = GetXBRL(ticker,PYear,"","mmGrossProfitMargin")
    if CurrentGPM>PriorGPM then A=1 else A=0 end

    local PQuarterInc0 = GetValueForQuarterOffset(ticker,1, "","mmIncome")
    local PQuarterInc1 = GetValueForQuarterOffset(ticker,2, "","mmIncome")
    local PQuarterInc2 = GetValueForQuarterOffset(ticker,3, "","mmIncome")
    local PQuarterInc3 = GetValueForQuarterOffset(ticker,4, "","mmIncome")
```

```
Income = PQuarterInc0+PQuarterInc1+PQuarterInc2+PQuarterInc3
if Income>0 then B=1 else B=0 end

local ROA=GetXBRLLatest(ticker,"","mmReturnOnAssets")
if ROA>0 then C=1 else C=0 end

local PQuarterOCF0 = GetValueForQuarterOffset(ticker,1, "","NetCashProvidedByUsedInOperatingActivities")
local PQuarterOCF1 = GetValueForQuarterOffset(ticker,2, "","NetCashProvidedByUsedInOperatingActivities")
local PQuarterOCF2 = GetValueForQuarterOffset(ticker,3, "","NetCashProvidedByUsedInOperatingActivities")
local PQuarterOCF3 = GetValueForQuarterOffset(ticker,4, "","NetCashProvidedByUsedInOperatingActivities")
OCF = PQuarterOCF0+PQuarterOCF1+PQuarterOCF2+PQuarterOCF3
if OCF>0 then D=1 else D=0 end

if OCF>Income then E=1 else E=0 end

local LongTermDebt=GetXBRLLatest(ticker,"","LongTermDebtNoncurrent")
local LongTermDebtCurrent=GetXBRLLatest(ticker,"","LongTermDebtCurrent")
local LongTermDebtPY = GetXBRL(ticker,PYear,"","LongTermDebtNoncurrent")
local LongTermDebtCurrentPY = GetXBRL(ticker,PYear,"","LongTermDebtCurrent")
if (LongTermDebt+LongTermDebtCurrent)<(LongTermDebtPY+LongTermDebtCurrentPY) then F=1 else F=0 end

local CurrentAssets=GetXBRLLatest(ticker,"","AssetsCurrent")
local CurrentLiabilities=GetXBRLLatest(ticker,"","LiabilitiesCurrent")
local CurrentAssetsPY = GetXBRL(ticker,PYear,"","AssetsCurrent")
local CurrentLiabilitiesPY = GetXBRL(ticker,PYear,"","LiabilitiesCurrent")
if (CurrentAssets/CurrentLiabilities)>(CurrentAssetsPY/CurrentLiabilitiesPY) then G=1 else G=0 end
local CurrentShares=GetXBRLLatest(ticker,"","mmSharesOutstanding")
local PriorShares = GetXBRL(ticker,PYear,"","mmSharesOutstanding")
if CurrentShares<PriorShares then H=1 else H=0 end

local Assets1=GetXBRLLatest(ticker,"","mmAssets")
local Assets2 = GetXBRL(ticker,PYear,"","mmAssets")
local Assets3 = GetXBRL(ticker,TwoYears,"","mmAssets")

local PQuarterInc0 = GetValueForQuarterOffset(ticker,1, "","mmRevenue")
local PQuarterInc1 = GetValueForQuarterOffset(ticker,2, "","mmRevenue")
local PQuarterInc2 = GetValueForQuarterOffset(ticker,3, "","mmRevenue")
local PQuarterInc3 = GetValueForQuarterOffset(ticker,4, "","mmRevenue")
TTMRevenue = PQuarterInc0+PQuarterInc1+PQuarterInc2+PQuarterInc3
local PQuarterInc4 = GetValueForQuarterOffset(ticker,5, "","mmRevenue")
local PQuarterInc5 = GetValueForQuarterOffset(ticker,6, "","mmRevenue")
local PQuarterInc6 = GetValueForQuarterOffset(ticker,7, "","mmRevenue")
local PQuarterInc7 = GetValueForQuarterOffset(ticker,8, "","mmRevenue")
TwoRevenue = PQuarterInc4+PQuarterInc5+PQuarterInc6+PQuarterInc7

CurrentAT = TTMRevenue/(Assets1+Assets2)
PriorAT = TwoRevenue/(Assets2+Assets3)

if CurrentAT>PriorAT then I=1 else I=0 end

Score = A+B+C+D+E+F+G+H+I

PrintLn("PiortroskiScore for this company is: "..Score)
PrintLn("A score of 8 or 9 indicates a high quality company, a score between 0-2 is considered weak")
PrintLn("A score of 1.8 or lower signals poor credit")
```

MY INVESTING STYLE

We learned about some of the popular stock-picking techniques in the previous three chapters, and I did mention that it is not how I pick stocks. So the time has come to explain my way of picking stocks and the use of scripting to do so. I emphasize that it is just my way of doing it and there are no guarantees that this is a good method or that it works or anything like that. I can only say that it is how I approach investing. Also, I would like to add that you might get disappointed since it is not as universal and as "easy" as you maybe hoped for.

Here is my general investment cycle:

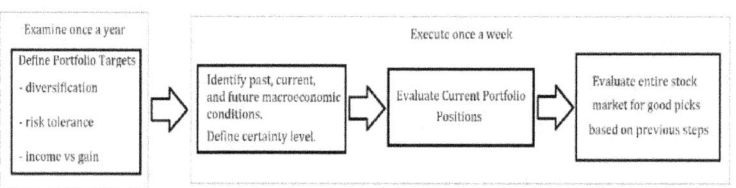

I start by examining my portfolio targets. Usually, I do it once a year or once every couple of years. I answer questions such as the following. How diversified do I want my portfolio to be? How stable is my and my family's situation? Maybe next year I can afford a bit more risk? Do I want a more steady income or am I interested in a growth portfolio? Answering these questions can help set generic portfolio targets. After this step, you should ideally be able to measure your risk tolerance measured in portfolio max drawdown. You should be able to get a portfolio composition target for diversification (from zero to one) and income/growth measured in percent of the portfolio. By the way, by "income" I usually mean either bonds or stocks with high dividends. I do not use scripts for this step. It is just a deep thinking step which I usually do alone while walking in the park.

I do the other three stages of the investing process weekly and I do use scripts to automate some of the laborious steps. I start with analyzing global economic conditions. Here is a non-exhaustive list of things I do to achieve macroeconomic awareness:

- Watch various news reports, including short CNBC/Bloomberg videos they put on YouTube
- Read various economic news articles for in-depth awareness
- Check Tickernomics Insight Charts sections to look for the updated charts of global economic parameters such as interest rates, money velocity, M2 money supply, etc.
- Check S&P500 charts, bond yield charts, volatility charts, commodity prices charts, etc.
- Watch out for any geopolitical risks that arise in the form of political and global news
- If I have time, I love watching interviews with prominent economics figures, SEC and federal reserve people, billionaires

I'm a visual person and charts tell me much more than just updated numbers, as I can see the context. The list above seems like a chore, but in reality, a lot of people spend many hours on useless news content, so just redirecting the emphasis to economic news can keep you better prepared while not taking more of your personal time. **You have to understand the world's overall state on a weekly basis to be a good investor.** For example, anecdotally in 2022, the US's gradual shift away from economic cooperation with China had a huge impact on Chinese stock prices. If recent news from China is concerning, maybe I do not want anything to do with Chinese stocks. So you simply cannot ignore politics when investing. I also love to take notes and then compare the notes I made from a few months back to my current observations because human memory is weak and I sometimes find myself surprised at my reactions to certain events just a few months back that I completely forgot. The comparison of past and present macroeconomic situations gives you a better investing perspective. Finally, for this step, I try to foresee what the global economic environment will look like in the future to achieve the final vision for macroeconomics. It is not easy to reliably predict what will happen, but it is still a good exercise because every time you are wrong with your predictions you learn how to be better at it and also how to protect yourself next time from unexpected surprises.

Once the macro-economy is figured out, I move to evaluate my current portfolio positions. I organize my portfolio into about 50 more or less equal slots. So I buy and sell positions into these slots. I try to keep about 50 different positions, which ensures I am decently diversified. A fixed size of a slot allows for easier management of positions and helps with certain math calculations. Sometimes a position can occupy multiple slots, but most of my positions occupy just one slot.

The problem of being overweight in a certain position can be solved by selling one of several slots that this position occupies. It is easier to visually identify overweight and underweight positions when you deal with slots of approximately equal size, because for us, humans, it is easier to compare 2 slots to 3 slots than to compare some arbitrary position sizes measured in dollars. Keeping these slots also helps with the fees I pay for transactions because if a slot is of a significant size then fees for taking or releasing a slot shouldn't be that big percentage-wise.

I use the three scripts to do portfolio analysis, which are all available in public scripts on Tickernomics (not a full list and constantly changing):

☐ PortfolioNegativesToSell (described earlier in the book and it searches for poorly performing positions that are also in a "hopeless state" so ranking them to be sold)

☐ PortfolioPositivesToSell (described earlier in the book and it searches for well-performing positions that are also in a "reached the top state" so ranking them to be sold)

☐ FindDivSafelyInPositions (I use this script to search within my positions for good dividend sources and I use that to consider adding to an existing position)

At this point, I do manual research on the top picks in the above scripts for consideration of selling some of the positions. Notice I do not consider buying or adding to positions yet. The manual research includes the following:

1. Full DCF (discounted cash flow) analysis of the position
2. Manual research of all three financial statements of the position
3. Look through certain charts of the position (price chart,

debt, revenue, income, and many more)

4. Reading specific news relevant to the position

If the manual research convinces me of selling one or more slots occupied by the position then I execute the transaction.

Then I move to the next phase in my approach, which is to look through the stock market for decent stock picks. During this phase (since I do all these steps on the same day) I keep the research I did in the previous step for the existing positions in mind. Looking through thousands of potential stock picks can only be done with pre-screening which is also done by scripting. I use the following scripts (not a full list and constantly changing):

☐ GARPStocks (we will see it in the next chapter)

☐ FindDivSafely3 (we saw it earlier)

☐ BenjaminGrahamNetNetStocks (we saw it earlier)

☐ Top10RevenueStatic (we will see it in the later chapters)

☐ CompaniesAtCyclicalHighs (we will see it in the next chapter)

I really like when multiple scripts highlight the same company. Then I get excited and start manual research on that company and the steps for manual research are almost identical to the steps I showed above for a portfolio position. The only difference is that the research is solely concentrated on answering the question of whether the stock is attractive enough for purchase rather than considering the selling as well.

During this phase, I also pay attention to stocks that show up in the script results and that I already own. After considering all the above, I make a decision to buy one or more slots of the stock that I found attractive.

So as you can see my approach is semi-automated and still involves a lot of manual research. It is not that time-consuming as I got used to it and a lot of steps are automated. In fact, the total time I spend managing my own portfolio is not more than 5 hours a week. It is totally manageable! Of course, I polished my style over the years and I do admit if someone starts it then at first it can take much more time...

26
MORE STOCK PICKING SCRIPTS

Why not learn a few more stock picking scripts?
GARPStocks script generates a vast list of Growth Stocks At
Reasonable Prices. This list can then be manually filtered to pick
some good choices. The filtering conditions used in this script
are:

- ☐ 5 Year revenue growth of at least 20% CAGR
- ☐ 3 Year FCF growth of at least 25% CAGR
- ☐ The current FCF Yield is at least 5%

The first two parameters identify the truly fast-growing
companies. The FCF Yield parameter is calculated as FCF
divided by the market capitalization of the company. If
capitalization is too high then FCF Yield will be very small hence
indicating the company is overvalued. So FCF Yield in a way is
similar to the PE ratio to identify overvalued companies. So the
GARPStocks script is an efficient tool to find fast-growing
companies that aren't too expensive. Here is the script:

```
local arr = {}
local arr1 = {}
local arr2 = {}
local arr3 = {}
local c=GetTickerCount()
local Labels=""
for i=0,c-1 do
  local ticker=GetTickerByIndex(i)

  --start of GARP formula. Conditions: 5 Year revenue growth at least 20% CAGR,
  --3 Year FCF growth at least 25% CAGR, and current FCF yield at least 5%
  local MarketCap = GetXBRLLatest(ticker,"","mmCapitalization")
  local FCFYield = GetXBRLLatest(ticker,"","mmFCFYieldAnnual")
  local CurrentRevenue = GetXBRLLatest(ticker,"","mmRevenueAnnual")
  local CurrentFCF = GetXBRLLatest(ticker,"","mmFCFAnnual")

  local today = GetTodayDay()
  local FiveYearsAgo = today - (5*365)
  local ThreeYearsAgo = today - (3*365)
  local FiveRevenue = GetXBRL(ticker,FiveYearsAgo,"","mmRevenueAnnual")
  local ThreeFCF = GetXBRL(ticker,ThreeYearsAgo,"","mmFCFAnnual")
```

```
if (FiveRevenue > 0) and (ThreeFCF > 0) and (CurrentFCF>0) and (CurrentRevenue>0) then
  FCFGrowth = (((CurrentFCF/ThreeFCF)^(1/3))-1)*100
  RevenueGrowth = (((CurrentRevenue/FiveRevenue)^(1/5))-1)*100
  --end of formula

  local Name=GetCompanyPropStr(ticker,"Name")
  if not isNaN(RevenueGrowth) then
      if FCFGrowth>25 and MarketCap>100 and RevenueGrowth>20 and FCFYield>5 then
          arr[Name]=RevenueGrowth --{ticker,rank}
          arr1[Name]=FCFGrowth --{ticker,rank}
          arr2[Name]=FCFYield --{ticker,rank}
          arr3[Name]=MarketCap --{ticker,rank}
      end
  end
end
end --for i
  local n=tablelength(arr)
  DeleteTable("GrowthAtAReasonablePriceStocks1")
  -- PrintLn(tickers)
  local i=0
  for k, v in pairs(arr) do
    if Labels ~= "" then
      Labels = Labels .. ","
    end
    Labels=Labels..k
    end
  CreateTable("GrowthAtAReasonablePriceStocks1",4,n,"RevenueGrowth,FCFGrowth,FCFYield,MarketCap",
  Labels,"RevenueGrowth");
    for k, v in pairs(arr) do
      local temp1 = arr1[k]
      local temp2 = arr2[k]
      local temp3 = arr3[k]
      if not isNaN(v) then
        SetTableValue("GrowthAtAReasonablePriceStocks1",0,i,v)
        SetTableValue("GrowthAtAReasonablePriceStocks1",1,i,temp1)
        SetTableValue("GrowthAtAReasonablePriceStocks1",2,i,temp2)
        SetTableValue("GrowthAtAReasonablePriceStocks1",3,i,temp3)
        i=i+1
      end
    end -- for k,v
  StoreTable("GrowthAtAReasonablePriceStocks1")
  PrintLn("Done generating list - Go to Insight Tables and select GrowthAtAReasonablePriceStocks"..
  "from the drop down list to see the list of stocks")
```

Another useful script mentioned in the previous chapter is CompaniesAtCyclicalHighs. This script's idea is also quite simple. We want to find companies with low PE ratios but operating margins significantly higher than the average for the previous periods. Thus, the low PE may be explained by the company's recent spike in profitability. The idea of this script is to identify companies that are "value traps" - a company that appears cheap based on historical valuation metrics, but may be cheap for a reason, such as operating margins returning to their historical average. However, it could also be used to find companies that recently experienced a spike in profitability where this new level may be the new norm, and thus the company may be undervalued.

The filtering criteria of the script:

- The P/E ratio is 10 or below
- Operating margin at least twice the 5-year average

Script source:

```
--Attributes: P/E ratio is 10 or below
--AND Operating margin last 12 months at least twice the 5 year average
function run()
    local arr1 = {}
    local arr2 = {}
    local arr3 = {}
    local arr4 = {}
    local c=GetTickerCount()
    local Labels=""
    for i=0,c-1 do
      local ticker=GetTickerByIndex(i)
      --start of dividend stocks formula
      -- local today = GetTodayDay()
      -- local TenYearsAgo = today - (10*365)
      local MarketCap = GetXBRLLatest(ticker,"","mmCapitalization")
      --Dividend yield
      local CurrentPE = GetXBRLLatest(ticker,"","mmPE")
      --Operating income last 12 months
      local PQuarterOI0 = GetValueForQuarterOffset(ticker,1, "","OperatingIncomeLoss")
      local PQuarterFOI1 = GetValueForQuarterOffset(ticker,2, "","OperatingIncomeLoss")
      local PQuarterFOI2 = GetValueForQuarterOffset(ticker,3, "","OperatingIncomeLoss")
      local PQuarterFOI3 = GetValueForQuarterOffset(ticker,4, "","OperatingIncomeLoss")
      TTMOI = PQuarterOI0+PQuarterFOI1+PQuarterFOI2+PQuarterFOI3
      --Revenue last 12 months
      local PQuarterRev0 = GetValueForQuarterOffset(ticker,1, "","mmRevenue")
      local PQuarterRev1 = GetValueForQuarterOffset(ticker,2, "","mmRevenue")
      local PQuarterRev2 = GetValueForQuarterOffset(ticker,3, "","mmRevenue")
```

```
local PQuarterRev3 = GetValueForQuarterOffset(ticker,4, "","mmRevenue")
TTMRevenue = PQuarterRev0+PQuarterRev1+PQuarterRev2+PQuarterRev3

CurrentOM = (TTMOI/TTMRevenue)*100

--operating margin last 5 years
local PQuarterOM4 = GetValueForQuarterOffset(ticker,5, "","OperatingIncomeLoss")
local PQuarterOM5 = GetValueForQuarterOffset(ticker,6, "","OperatingIncomeLoss")
local PQuarterOM6 = GetValueForQuarterOffset(ticker,7, "","OperatingIncomeLoss")
local PQuarterOM7 = GetValueForQuarterOffset(ticker,8, "","OperatingIncomeLoss")

local PQuarterOM8 = GetValueForQuarterOffset(ticker,9, "","OperatingIncomeLoss")
local PQuarterOM9 = GetValueForQuarterOffset(ticker,10, "","OperatingIncomeLoss")
local PQuarterOM10 = GetValueForQuarterOffset(ticker,11, "","OperatingIncomeLoss")
local PQuarterOM11 = GetValueForQuarterOffset(ticker,12, "","OperatingIncomeLoss")

local PQuarterOM12 = GetValueForQuarterOffset(ticker,13, "","OperatingIncomeLoss")
local PQuarterOM13 = GetValueForQuarterOffset(ticker,14, "","OperatingIncomeLoss")
local PQuarterOM14 = GetValueForQuarterOffset(ticker,15, "","OperatingIncomeLoss")
local PQuarterOM15 = GetValueForQuarterOffset(ticker,16, "","OperatingIncomeLoss")

local PQuarterOM16 = GetValueForQuarterOffset(ticker,17, "","OperatingIncomeLoss")
local PQuarterOM17 = GetValueForQuarterOffset(ticker,18, "","OperatingIncomeLoss")
local PQuarterOM18 = GetValueForQuarterOffset(ticker,19, "","OperatingIncomeLoss")
local PQuarterOM19 = GetValueForQuarterOffset(ticker,20, "","OperatingIncomeLoss")
TotalFiveYearOM = TTMOI+PQuarterOM4+PQuarterOM5+PQuarterOM6+PQuarterOM7+PQuarterOM8+
PQuarterOM9+PQuarterOM10+PQuarterOM11+PQuarterOM12+PQuarterOM13+PQuarterOM14+PQuarterOM15+
PQuarterOM16+PQuarterOM17+PQuarterOM18+PQuarterOM19

    --Revenue last 5 years
local PQuarterRevenue4 = GetValueForQuarterOffset(ticker,5, "","mmRevenue")
local PQuarterRevenue5 = GetValueForQuarterOffset(ticker,6, "","mmRevenue")
local PQuarterRevenue6 = GetValueForQuarterOffset(ticker,7, "","mmRevenue")
local PQuarterRevenue7 = GetValueForQuarterOffset(ticker,8, "","mmRevenue")

local PQuarterRevenue8 = GetValueForQuarterOffset(ticker,9, "","mmRevenue")
local PQuarterRevenue9 = GetValueForQuarterOffset(ticker,10, "","mmRevenue")
local PQuarterRevenue10 = GetValueForQuarterOffset(ticker,11, "","mmRevenue")
local PQuarterRevenue11 = GetValueForQuarterOffset(ticker,12, "","mmRevenue")

local PQuarterRevenue12 = GetValueForQuarterOffset(ticker,13, "","mmRevenue")
local PQuarterRevenue13 = GetValueForQuarterOffset(ticker,14, "","mmRevenue")
local PQuarterRevenue14 = GetValueForQuarterOffset(ticker,15, "","mmRevenue")
local PQuarterRevenue15 = GetValueForQuarterOffset(ticker,16, "","mmRevenue")

local PQuarterRevenue16 = GetValueForQuarterOffset(ticker,17, "","mmRevenue")
local PQuarterRevenue17 = GetValueForQuarterOffset(ticker,18, "","mmRevenue")
local PQuarterRevenue18 = GetValueForQuarterOffset(ticker,19, "","mmRevenue")
local PQuarterRevenue19 = GetValueForQuarterOffset(ticker,20, "","mmRevenue")
TotalFiveYearRevenue = TTMRevenue+PQuarterRevenue4+PQuarterRevenue5+PQuarterRevenue6+
PQuarterRevenue7+PQuarterRevenue8+PQuarterRevenue9+PQuarterRevenue10+PQuarterRevenue11+
PQuarterRevenue12+PQuarterRevenue13+PQuarterRevenue14+PQuarterRevenue15+PQuarterRevenue16+
PQuarterRevenue17+PQuarterRevenue18+PQuarterRevenue19

FiveYearAverageOperatingMargin = (TotalFiveYearOM/TotalFiveYearRevenue)*100

OMRatio = CurrentOM/FiveYearAverageOperatingMargin
```

```
    local Name=GetCompanyPropStr(ticker,"Name")
    local Industry=GetCompanyPropStr(ticker,"Industry")
    if not isNaN(CurrentOM) and not isNaN(FiveYearAverageOperatingMargin) and MarketCap>50 and
CurrentPE<10 and CurrentPE>0.01 and OMRatio>1.99 and CurrentOM>0 and
        FiveYearAverageOperatingMargin>0 and Industry~="Banks-Regional" and Industry~="REIT-Mortgage"
and Industry~="Insurance-Diversified" and Industry~="Banks-Diversified"
        and Industry~="Insurance-Life" and Industry~="REIT-Office" and Industry~="Insurance-Specialty"
and Industry~="Mortgage Finance"
        --CurrentPE<10 and OMRatio>1.9 and
        then
            arr1[Name.."/ "..Industry]=CurrentPE  --{ticker,rank}
            arr2[Name.."/ "..Industry]=CurrentOM  --{ticker,rank}
            arr3[Name.."/ "..Industry]=FiveYearAverageOperatingMargin  --{ticker,rank}
            arr4[Name.."/ "..Industry]=MarketCap
        end
    end --i
local n=tablelength(arr1)
DeleteTable("CompaniesAtCyclicalHighs")
-- PrintLn(tickers)
local i=0
for k, v in pairs(arr1) do
    if Labels ~= "" then
      Labels = Labels .. ","
    end
    Labels=Labels..k
end
CreateTable("CompaniesAtCyclicalHighs",4,n,"PE Ratio,CurrentOperatingMargin,"..
"FiveYearAverageOperatingMargin,MarketCap",Labels,"PE Ratio");
    for k, v in pairs(arr1) do
      local temp2 = arr2[k]
      local temp3 = arr3[k]
      local temp4 = arr4[k]
      if not isNaN(v) then
        SetTableValue("CompaniesAtCyclicalHighs",0,i,v)
        SetTableValue("CompaniesAtCyclicalHighs",1,i,temp2)
        SetTableValue("CompaniesAtCyclicalHighs",2,i,temp3)
        SetTableValue("CompaniesAtCyclicalHighs",3,i,temp4)
        i=i+1
      end
    end -- for k,v
StoreTable("CompaniesAtCyclicalHighs")
PrintLn("Done finding Value Trap Stocks - Go to Insight Tables and select CompaniesAtCyclicalHighs"..
" from the drop down list to see the list of stocks")
```

The result of the script looks like this:

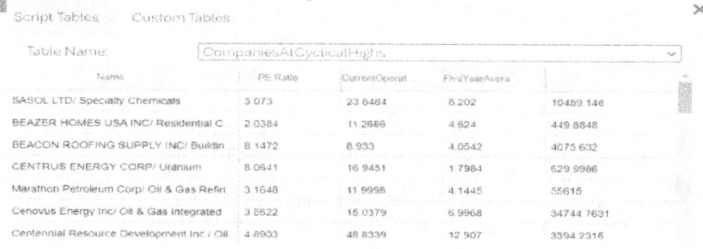

Name	PE Ratio	CurrentOperat...	FiveYearAvera...	
SASOL LTD/ Specialty Chemicals	3.073	23.6484	8.202	10489.146
BEAZER HOMES USA INC/ Residential C...	2.0384	11.2686	4.624	449.8848
BEACON ROOFING SUPPLY INC/ Buildin...	8.1472	8.933	4.0542	4075.632
CENTRUS ENERGY CORP/ Uranium	8.0641	16.9451	1.7984	629.9986
Marathon Petroleum Corp/ Oil & Gas Refin...	3.1648	11.9998	4.1445	55615
Cenovus Energy Inc/ Oil & Gas Integrated	3.8622	15.0379	6.9968	34744.7631
Centennial Resource Development Inc./ Oil...	4.8903	48.8339	12.907	3394.2316

Besides the scripts above, my other important approach
in investing via scripts is to do "a quick script to address the

news I just heard". What I mean by this can be explained by an example: I heard that tech companies are doing pretty badly in the year 2022. So I realized that the overall sentiment toward tech will be bad for a long time. Crowds' reaction to the tech downturn is uniform. So what do I do?

The best thing is to quickly write a tech-specific script that will scan hundreds of tech companies to identify ones that were hit too much and in reality should be valued higher. Of course, such a script would filter for tech companies out of all companies, but it can also perform an analysis that is specifically designed for tech companies .

In this tech company script, we will check for the following: revenue growth, goodwill growth just before the downturn (high growth in the goodwill balance would mean they were aggressively acquiring businesses and therefore will be hit especially hard if the value of those acquired businesses is suddenly much less than what they paid), accounts receivables vs accounts payables (high disparity might mean they were too aggressive bringing more customers to spark growth and now with the sudden downturn might be hit very hard), and of course growth in debt. Then I would build a total rank out of those parameters, one might call this rank - Aggressive Growth Rank, and if this rank is low for a tech company, but the stock dropped a lot together with other tech companies, I might identify this tech company as "oversold". So this is an example of me using the dedicated script to address a specific market situation. It proved to be quite effective for me.

In the next chapter, we will take a glimpse into some of the "dedicated" scripts designed to solve one specific problem.

27
DEDICATED SCRIPTS

Scripting doesn't have to be only about stock screening and portfolio management. Sometimes scripts can also help to understand the macroeconomy, a specific industry situation, or a specific company's intricate details. I will show some examples of so-called dedicated scripts. These scripts solve a specific problem that would be really hard to solve manually.

One important task an investor should always perform when preparing to invest in a company is to make sure the company is not going into bankruptcy any time soon. One approach that helps to numerically evaluate the probability of bankruptcy is the so-called liquidity analysis.

Liquidity analysis calculates how much or how long a company can survive on the liquid assets it has minus imminent expenses it must incur. This is very similar to analyzing a person's liquidity situation. A person might not be poor and might own a one million dollar house in Hawaii, but he might only have five thousand dollars in the bank and suddenly he is fired and he has a five thousand dollar mortgage payment coming due next month. He might face a liquidity problem. Most likely such a person will find a solution but if for some reason he doesn't he might default on his mortgage with horrible consequences. So a liquidity analysis is not the most important thing to understand about a company when conducting research, but it is still a good practice to do, just in case. This analysis might be especially important if you as an investor expect a sharp downturn in the overall economy and you want to make sure the company won't mess up its finances during a crisis.

We can analyze the liquidity of companies by using liquidity ratios and analyzing how many days are needed to sell inventory, receive payment from customers, and pay suppliers for the purchase of inventory.

Here is the list of parameters we often use to measure liquidity:

- Current Ratio = Current Assets divided by Current Liabilities. If above 1 then it means that current assets easily exceed current liabilities and we shouldn't have liquidity issues in general, unless current assets are predominantly made up of inventory which the company is having trouble selling.

- Quick Ratio = Cash, Investments, Net Accounts Receivables divided by Current Liabilities. It is in my opinion a better ratio because it has all the immediately available money in the numerator and the expenses coming due in 1 year or less in the denominator.

- Days Sales Outstanding (DSO) - is the average number of days it takes for a company to receive payment for a sale. Also referred to as accounts receivable collection period.

- Days Inventory Outstanding (DIO) - is a working capital management ratio that measures the average number of days that a company holds inventory before turning it into sales.

- Days Payables Outstanding (DPO) - is a financial ratio that indicates the average time (in days) that a company takes to pay its bills and invoices to its trade creditors.

DSO is calculated by dividing average net accounts receivables by sales and prorating by 365 days in a year.

Similarly, DIO is calculated by dividing the average inventory by the cost of revenue and multiplying by 365 days.

Finally, DPO is calculated by dividing accounts payable by the cost of revenue and multiplying by 365 days.

The script generating liquidity measures above:

```
--Liquidity Ratios: Current, Quick, Days Sales O/S, Days O/S Inventory,
--Days Payables O/S, cash conversion cycle

--define current assets, current liabilities, and calculate the current ratio
local CurrentAssets = GetXBRLLatest(ticker,"","AssetsCurrent")
local CurrentLiabilities = GetXBRLLatest(ticker,"","LiabilitiesCurrent")
CurrentRatio = CurrentAssets/CurrentLiabilities

--define cash and investments, accounts receivable(AR) and calculate the quick ratio
local CashAndInvestments = GetXBRLLatest(ticker,"","InvestmentsAndCash")
local AR = GetXBRLLatest(ticker,"","AccountsReceivableNetCurrent")
QuickRatio = (CashAndInvestments+AR)/CurrentLiabilities

--define cash flow from operations for the past 12 months
local CurrentOCF = GetXBRLLatest(ticker,"","NetCashProvidedByUsedInOperatingActivities")
local SecondOCF = GetValueForQuarterOffset(ticker,2, "", "NetCashProvidedByUsedInOperatingActivities")
local ThirdOCF = GetValueForQuarterOffset(ticker,3, "", "NetCashProvidedByUsedInOperatingActivities")
local FourthOCF = GetValueForQuarterOffset(ticker,4, "", "NetCashProvidedByUsedInOperatingActivities")
TotalOCF = CurrentOCF+SecondOCF+ThirdOCF+FourthOCF

--define OCF to current liabilities ratio
OCFtoCurrentLiabilities = TotalOCF/CurrentLiabilities

--define prior year
local today = GetTodayDay()
local PYear = today - 365
--Days Sales Outstanding
local Revenue = GetXBRLLatest(ticker,"","mmRevenueAnnual")
local PYearAR = GetXBRL(ticker,PYear,"","AccountsReceivableNetCurrent")
DSO = (((AR+PYearAR)/2)/Revenue)*365

--Days Inventory Outstanding
local CurrentInventory = GetXBRLLatest(ticker,"","InventoryNet")
local PInventory = GetXBRL(ticker,PYear,"","InventoryNet")
local CurrentCOGS = GetXBRLLatest(ticker,"","mmCostOfRevenue")
local SecondCOGS = GetValueForQuarterOffset(ticker,2, "", "mmCostOfRevenue")
local ThirdCOGS = GetValueForQuarterOffset(ticker,3, "", "mmCostOfRevenue")
local FourthCOGS = GetValueForQuarterOffset(ticker,4, "", "mmCostOfRevenue")
TotalCOGS=CurrentCOGS+SecondCOGS+ThirdCOGS+FourthCOGS
DIO = (((CurrentInventory+PInventory)/2)/TotalCOGS)*365

--Days Payables Outstanding
local CurrentAP = GetXBRLLatest(ticker,"","AccountsPayableCurrent")
local PriorAP = GetXBRL(ticker,PYear,"","AccountsPayableCurrent")
DPO = (((CurrentAP+PriorAP)/2)/TotalCOGS)*365

--cash conversion cycle
CCC=DSO+DIO-DPO
```

The result:

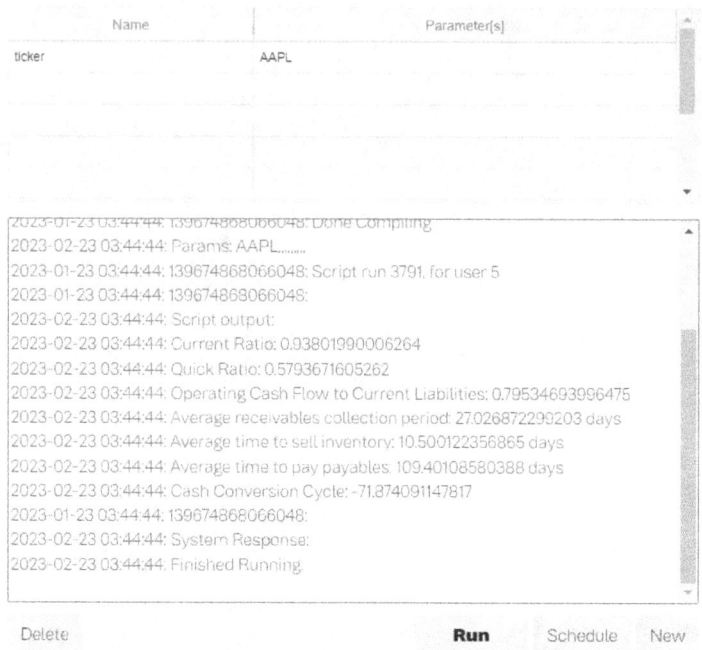

Liquidity is important for assessing the immediate financial risks to the company, but what about the assessment of the general health of the company? Solvency ratios assess those risks:

- Debt/Equity
- Debt/Assets
- Equity/Assets
- EBIT/Interest
- EBITDA/Interest

Here is the script that calculates them:

```
--define debt
local TotalDebt = GetXBRLLatest(ticker,"","Liabilities")
local TotalAssets = GetXBRLLatest(ticker,"","mmAssets")
local TotalEquity = GetXBRLLatest(ticker,"","mmBookValue")

--define debt/equity and debt/assets ratios
DERatio = TotalDebt/TotalEquity
DARatio = TotalDebt/TotalAssets
EARatio = TotalEquity/TotalAssets

--define total depreciation ttm
local DA = GetXBRLLatest(ticker,"","DepreciationAndAmortization")
local SecondDA = GetValueForQuarterOffset(ticker,2, "", "DepreciationAndAmortization")
local ThirdDA = GetValueForQuarterOffset(ticker,3, "", "DepreciationAndAmortization")
local FourthDA = GetValueForQuarterOffset(ticker,4, "", "DepreciationAndAmortization")
TotalDA = DA+SecondDA+ThirdDA+FourthDA

--define operating income ttm
local OperatingIncome = GetXBRLLatest(ticker,"","OperatingIncomeLoss")
local SecondOperatingIncome = GetValueForQuarterOffset(ticker,2, "", "OperatingIncomeLoss")
local ThirdOperatingIncome = GetValueForQuarterOffset(ticker,3, "", "OperatingIncomeLoss")
local FourthOperatingIncome = GetValueForQuarterOffset(ticker,4, "", "OperatingIncomeLoss")
TotalOI = OperatingIncome+SecondOperatingIncome+ThirdOperatingIncome+FourthOperatingIncome

--define EBITDA ttm
EBITDA=TotalOI+TotalDA

--define interest expense
local InterestExpense = GetXBRLLatest(ticker,"","InterestExpense")
local SecondInterestExpense = GetValueForQuarterOffset(ticker,2, "", "InterestExpense")
local ThirdInterestExpense = GetValueForQuarterOffset(ticker,3, "", "InterestExpense")
local FourthInterestExpense = GetValueForQuarterOffset(ticker,4, "", "InterestExpense")
TotalInterestExpense = InterestExpense+SecondInterestExpense+ThirdInterestExpense+FourthInterestExpense

--define EBIT to interest ratio and EBITDA to interest ratio
EBITtoInterest = TotalOI/TotalInterestExpense
EBITDAtoInterest = EBITDA/TotalInterestExpense

--print outputs
PrintLn("Debt/Equity: "..DERatio)
PrintLn("Debt/Assets: "..DARatio)
PrintLn("Equity/Assets: "..EARatio)
PrintLn("EBIT/Interest: "..EBITtoInterest)
PrintLn("EBITDA/Interest: "..EBITDAtoInterest)
```

There are many more specialized scripts one can design. The typical company reports hundreds of parameters every quarter. Every reported number brings additional detail to the full picture of the company's state. The reported numbers accumulate over the years as a company conducts its business. In addition to that, there are various news reports by the news agencies about a company; there are analysts digging for more information on every company, etc, etc. The companies form clusters as they don't independently exist but interact with each other. A human being cannot process those volumes of information, but it all can be analyzed in full totality by properly designed scripts.

28
TRICKY BUSINESS

The size of a company matters. You probably noticed that most scripts in the previous chapters had a condition that company capitalization should be above 50 million or 100 million. The reason for that is to filter out tiny companies. A public company with a capitalization below 100 million is truly tiny. Think about it. 100 million is not much in today's world. If you take a walk down the street in any urban or suburban city, you will probably walk by more than 100 million worth in real estate. You are dealing with a public company of that size. The company has to have a board of directors, file SEC documents, and manage all that stuff that the law requires public companies to manage, yet the company is tiny and has to maintain all that public company overhead.

Hostile takeovers and manipulations are common. There are thousands of private equity funds, investment companies, and activist funds that browse the market for tiny companies all the time. Many of those funds buy several companies of 100 million or so in size every year. What do you think happens with tiny companies like that in terms of shareholder composition? Many of these small public companies have a huge number of their shareholders coming from those funds. That means one word for you – politics. There are many ways in which big investors can screw up a small public company. The most popular approach is to vote the "right people" into the board of directors for the tiny company so you can manipulate company decisions. Sometimes these decisions can intentionally lower the stock price of the company so the interested party can buy the whole company really cheaply and then remove it from the public stock market. Another thing the "right people" can do is to siphon money out of the public company into private LLCs owned by other "right people" via lucrative contracts between a public company and those private LLCs.

So now the question for you – an honest investor without the internal knowledge of these small public companies: do you really want to deal with all that politics? I don't. So that is the real reason why I never invest in small public companies. I stick with mid to large cap cause it is way harder to push special interests in a giant company with a wide distribution of investors.

Unfortunately, that is how it used to be. I am getting concerned about the state of the public stock market. The reason for that is the systemic shift towards passive investing strategies by the majority of investors in recent decades. A combination of factors including people lacking time, advances in computer systems, cultural changes, the invention of advanced investment instruments, promotion, and ads all push people to switch from being active investors into passive ones. The biggest factor is the growth of mutual funds, index funds, and low-cost ETFs.

If a person invests in mutual funds, index funds, or ETFs he is told that he is well protected to weather the storm since his investment is diversified and well managed by professionals. It might be true, but there is one problem. Such investors just traded convenience for his freedom, quite literally. An individual investor who switched to ETFs will not vote for board members of companies when they are hidden behind ETF or index fund facades. Someone else will vote for board members instead of such lazy investors. Seems like not a big deal. And indeed it is not a big deal for one investor, but what we are seeing in modern times is that the majority of individual investors are invested in assets that do not allow them to vote for board members in the companies. This spawned a tectonic cultural shift...

I would say around 10-20% of the voting power of most S&P500 companies is in hands of BlackRock and Vanguard managers. That is enough of a concentration of voting power to have significant control on most companies' strategic management because the voting power for the rest of the stockholders is spread across many diverse minor investors in most cases and they cannot synchronously vote for the right guy. Remember that a lot of individual stockholders also ignore voting mail and don't cast their vote, but BlackRock people sure do. So just like with political voting, I encourage all individual investors to vote thoughtfully for the boards because it is shaping America maybe even more than political voting.

Those large ETF issuers and the mutual funds have enormous control over corporate America. This kind of voting power destroys the foundation of capitalism since there is no guarantee that the investors will control companies for **their best interests**. If in previous decades politics was a risk for small public companies, these days all public companies are at risk of politics and manipulations on a grand scale.

There is another systemic risk ETFs bring to the table. By law, not all underlying assets of ETFs can be in the ETF issuer's possession... There are some limits that make it safe, but my concern is that over time they might allow much looser underlying assets limits and then we might see the Black Swan event when suddenly there will be too many ETFs, but not enough underlying assets to cover them. Let's hope this never happens.

One of the reasons for writing this book was to encourage the return of individual investors to active strategies and if I manage to help at least some people in making the right choice I would consider my mission a success. One might ask what is the point of being an active investor if the market is "fixed". It is not actually true that the entire market is "fixed". Only some percent of stocks might be manipulated at any given time, at least for now... There are three ways one handles this problem. The first way is to spot manipulations, but this goes beyond the content of this book. The second way is diversification such that you can only be hit by manipulation at a tiny percentage of your assets. The third way is to avoid small and even medium-sized companies.

Another new risk one should consider is the "meme stocks" risk. When running the scripts and doing proper value investing, one might completely overlook the fact that the company you decide to invest in was recently popularized by some blogger with ten million subscribers, or by some celebrity on TV. So it is very important to check all the news about your stock pick before investing in order to not get into one of those psychological traps.

Finally, it is beneficial to analyze insider's actions with the company stocks as well as funds ownership of the stock. For that, we can use some scripting. The first script below prints AAPL's recent insider transactions:

```
function run()
  for i=0,1000,1 do
    local trType = GetInsiderInfo("AAPL",i,"TrType")
    if trType~="" then
      local person = GetInsiderInfo("AAPL",i,"Person")
      local position = GetInsiderInfo("AAPL",i,"Position")
      local trDate = GetInsiderInfo("AAPL",i,"ExecuteDate")
      local trAmount = GetInsiderInfo("AAPL",i,"Amount")
      PrintLn(trType .. " " ..trDate .." ".. trAmount.." "..person .. " " .. position)
    end
  end
end
```

The printout looks like this:

S 2021-11-11 1350750.00 KONDO CHRIS Principal Accounting Officer
S 2021-11-11 1350750.00 Chris Kondo
A 2021-11-08 0.00 Gorsky Alex
S 2021-10-31 3717000.00 Katherine L Adams
S 2021-10-31 490572.00 Adams Katherine L. SVP, GC and Secretary
S 2021-10-18 24645500.00 Maestri Luca Senior Vice President, CFO
S 2021-10-18 24645505.98 Luca Maestri
S 2021-10-17 2670448.45 Deirdre O'brien
S 2021-10-17 167148.00 O'BRIEN DEIRDRE Senior Vice President

"S" stands for selling transactions and "A" for acquisitions. Insider transactions can also be viewed in the "Companies" feature by selecting a company and going to the "Insiders" tab. As you can see there was a lot of selling by insiders for Apple stock at the end of 2021, which is exactly when the long-term growth trend for Apple was broken. It seems sometimes it is just enough to look at what insiders are doing.

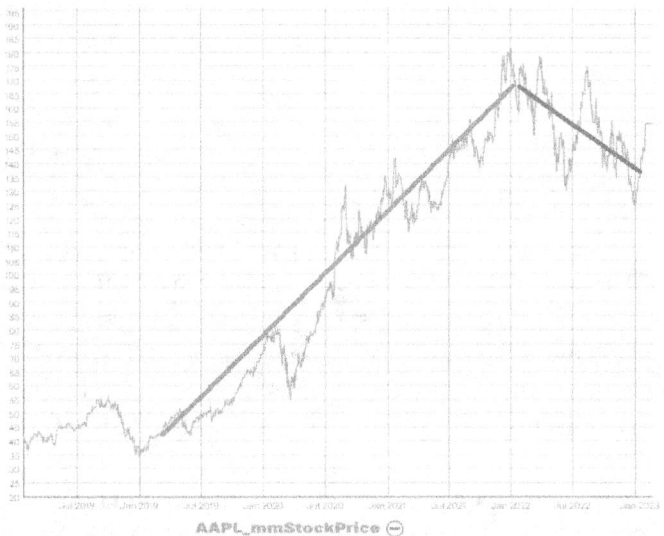

AAPL_mmStockPrice ⊖

The other important indicator is how much ownership of the stock is in the hands of funds, and even more important

215

how this ownership changes over time.

Here is the script that prints funds ownership for AAPL:

```
function run()
  local ticker="AAPL"
  local today=GetTodayDay()
  for i=0,10,1 do
    local owner=GetFundInfo(ticker,today,i,"EntityProperName")
    local amount=GetFundInfo(ticker,today,i,"ReportedHolding")
    PrintLn(owner .. " " .. amount)
  end
end
```

The result:

```
Fisher Asset Management, LLC 59176198
Royal Bank of Canada 56604627
Vanguard Group Inc 1272378901
Berkshire Hathaway Inc 894802319
State Street Corporation 591543874
Goldman Sachs Group Inc 81857956
Swiss National Bank 70142608
Wellington Management Company LLP 67208273
Bank of New York Mellon Corp 136302871
FMR Inc 350900116
```

Notice we used the GetTodayDay function to retrieve fund ownership for today. You can actually use an older date as an input and retrieve the fund ownership from a year ago which can provide an interesting perspective on which funds increased their Apple ownership and which ones decreased it. You can also review the current fund ownership data in the "Companies" feature by selecting a company and going to the "Funds" tab.

This was an unusual chapter for investment books that probably made you a bit concerned about the state of affairs in public stock investments. I am still excited about the opportunities that the stock market offers despite all the concerns.

29
REPORTS AND INTEGRATIONS

So far we have been learning things that would help us with investment decisions, but what about the practicalities? You are a busy person and you might want something automated so you save time for other things in life. Or maybe you are a finance professional and you want to integrate your existing computer systems with the scripting results. In any case, this chapter is going to teach you various ways of integrating, automating and generating investment reports using scripts. This chapter is somewhat technical but learning the material in it can help you a lot to streamline your research process.

We mentioned a lot of portfolio management techniques before. A portfolio is formed by entering transactions, but how can you bring your existing transactions into Tickernomics to analyze your portfolio? You might have executed transactions on various trading platforms and banks. Most of the platforms allow you to export your transaction data in tabular form. The most popular formats are Excel and CSV. If you have Excel you can easily save the excel file in CSV format. So eventually you will have a bunch of CSV files from different trading platforms where you do your investments. This is the time when we can write a small script to be able to import CSV files into Tickernomics (It is available in Public Scripts and it is called ImportTransactions).

A typical CSV file looks like this:

```
1,2021-08-10,SSYS,5,70.2,bought stratasys
2,2021-09-12,SSYS,4,75.9,sold stratasys
```

Each new line is a new row and commas separate column values for that row. In the example above we have a specific format determining what each column means. The first column is transaction type where 1 means "buy" and 2 means "sell". Then we have the transaction date. After the next comma, we have the ticker symbol and then the number of stocks. Finally we have a price and a comment. Of course, your trading platform will export CSV in a different format so each column will mean something else and then it will be your job to modify the script below to properly process each row:

```
function run(list)
    local i=0;
    for word in string.gmatch(list, '([^,]+)') do
        i = i + 1
        if (i==1) then
            SetTransactionValue(0,'TransactionType',word)
        end
        if (i==2) then
            SetTransactionValueStr(0,'TransactionDate',word)
        end
        if (i==3) then
            SetTransactionValueStr(0,'Ticker',word)
        end
        if (i==4) then
            SetTransactionValue(0,'Qty',word)
        end
        if (i==5) then
            SetTransactionValue(0,'UnitPrice',word)
        end
        if (i==6) then
            SetTransactionValueStr(0,'Note',word)
            i=0
            StoreTransaction(0)
        end
    end
end
```

You are already familiar with SetTransactionValue and StoreTransaction commands to add a transaction. The tricky part in the script above is:

```
string.gmatch(list, '([^,]+)')
```

The string.gmatch command takes as the first argument any text and as the second argument it takes a special selection expression. string.gmatch returns a list of the expression matches in the text. The expression format is called RegEx. You can learn about this format outside of this book as it is a very popular and extensive subject. The one thing to note about the expression:

The comma is what we search for and ^ means we search for the start of the string.

The script iterates through all matches which will be all the matches for all the commas in CSV. So checking "i==number" we determine which column it is and set the value for that column in a transaction. That is the part you will need to change based on the CSV file format of your trading platform.

Once you have modified the script accordingly you can run it and use it as input for the CSV text from your trading platforms. The script will create all the transactions for you and you won't need to manually enter them. This saves time and is very helpful in the long run especially if you have multiple trading platforms.

Everyone knows that generating reports to superiors or customers is part of the life of most finance professionals. If you need to generate a report that all your customers need to see you can do it directly in Tickernomics using scripting. There are a few advantages that reports in Tickernomics provide:

- Charts and Tables in Tickernomics reports are "live"
- The reports can be regenerated automatically weekly
- Reports can become searchable by search engines

☐ You can place financial data from scripts directly into reports without intermediates

For example, the following script generates a report for the Top 10 Latest Revenue Growth companies (i.e., the companies with the highest revenue growth when comparing their most recent quarterly revenue to their 400 day moving average for quarterly revenue). It is presented as so-called Static Content. So the report will have its own unique permanent link and you can share it with your customers. Search engines like Google will also be able to find it so it can be perfect for some kind of blogging report as well(the code is on the next page).

If you run the script then the script result will be accessible anywhere in the world via permalink: https://www.tickernomics.com/static/Top%2010%20Latest%20Revenue%20Growth .

The generated contents are a normal web page! You can generate your own HTML web pages using scripting.

HTML documents are organized hierarchically, as a tree-like structure of tags/nodes. A tag/node is an element inside of the HTML document that serves a specific purpose. The most common types of tags/nodes are: a paragraph(p), a header(h1), a picture(img), a list (ul) etc. The root node of an HTML document is its blank body where various tags can be placed. There is a special type of a tag called "div". Those don't do anything except to serve as containers that have more tags inside of them. So you can have a div tag in the body of an HTML document and this div tag can contain more paragraph tags or a picture, etc.

```
local name="Top 10 Latest Revenue Growth"
ClearStaticPage(name)
local idHeader=AddToStaticPage(name,"","div","font-size:16px;height: 4rem;width:100%;",
   "Quarterly report of the Top 10 companies that saw their revenue grow a lot ".. 
   "relative to their 400 day running average.")
local idBody=AddToStaticPage(name,"","div",
   "margin-top:1rem;height: calc(100% - 2rem);width:100%;","")
local idTable=AddToStaticPage(name,idBody,"table","width:100%;height:100%","")
local idHead=AddToStaticPage(name,idTable,"tr","","")
AddToStaticPage(name,idHead,"td","","Ticker")
AddToStaticPage(name,idHead,"td","","Name")
AddToStaticPage(name,idHead,"td","","Revenue Growth %")

local tickerTotal=GetTickerCount()
local arr = {}
local i=0;
for i=0,tickerTotal,1
do
   local ticker=GetTickerByIndex(i)

   local latestV=GetXBRLLatest(ticker,"","mmRevenue");
   local avgV=GetXBRLLatest(ticker,"","avg400mmRevenue");
   if avgV > 0 then
     if latestV > avgV then
       local perc=math.floor(100.0*(latestV-avgV)/latestV)
       if perc < 5000 then --cut off crazy ones
         arr[ticker]= perc --{ticker,divid}
       end
     end
   end
   i=i+1
end--tickers

local sortedKeys = getKeysSortedByValue(arr, function(a, b) return a > b end)

local n=10
local result="";
for _, key in ipairs(sortedKeys) do
   local idR=AddToStaticPage(name,idTable,"tr","","")
   AddToStaticPage(name,idR,"td","",key)
   local comp=GetCompanyPropStr(key,"Name")
   AddToStaticPage(name,idR,"td","",comp)
   AddToStaticPage(name,idR,"td","",arr[key])
   PrintLn(key .. " " .. arr[key]);
   --result=result..", " .. key .. " " .. arr[key]
   n=n-1
   if n <=0 then break end
end
```

The contents of the results were built using just one new
command that you need to learn: AddToStaticPage. This
command has a lot of arguments though. Here is the explanation
of all the arguments:

☐ PageName – the name of the page. It can have a "/"
symbol to create folders. For example, you can name a

folder after your name and the page name will be after your name like so: "myname/mypage1".

- [ ] TagParentId – the content is added to the parent node. If you specify nothing then the content is added to the root of your report.

- [ ] TagType – determines the type of the tag. The tag can be "div", "h2", "p" etc. Pretty much all tags allowed in HTML format are allowed.

- [ ] Style – this is a CSS format string

- [ ] Content – this is the text that goes into the tag contents.

Teaching you HTML/CSS format goes beyond this book, but it is the world's standard for displaying web content. It is a very simple format to learn and even kids can do their own web pages, so there is nothing to be afraid of here. Just watch some introduction videos to HTML/CSS and you should be good to start playing with it.

Finally, I would like to show to you how to add live charts and tables to HTML reports. Take a look at the following script:

```
function run()
    ClearStaticPage("LiveChartandTableDemo")
    AddToStaticPageCSS("LiveChartandTableDemo",".statictable tr td","border: 1px solid;")
    AddToStaticPage("LiveChartandTableDemo","","h4","","Live Chart and Table Demo")
    local divChart=AddToStaticPage("LiveChartandTableDemo","","div","width:100%;height: 600px;","")
    AddToStaticPagePermaContent("LiveChartandTableDemo",
        divChart,"/permchart.html?params=eyJjaGFydE5hbWUiOiJNU0ZUX21tU3RvY2mljZSJ9")
    local divTable=AddToStaticPage("LiveChartandTableDemo","","div","width:100%;height: 400px;","")
    AddToStaticPagePermaContent("LiveChartandTableDemo",divTable,
        "/perma/table?name=NWhoV2ZvaU1ybnBIbXxsaWdyang1")
end
```

We call ClearStaticPage to clear previous web pages with the same name if such existed. Then we use the AddToStaticPageCSS command which adds CSS styling to the HTML class "statictable". In this case, we define a solid border with a 1-pixel thickness. We call AddToStaticPage to add an HTML H4 tag with the page title. Then we use AddToStaticPagePermaContent. This call embeds into the web page content from another URL on Tickernomics. In this case, we created a table and a chart earlier and got their perma-links which are usually accessible here:

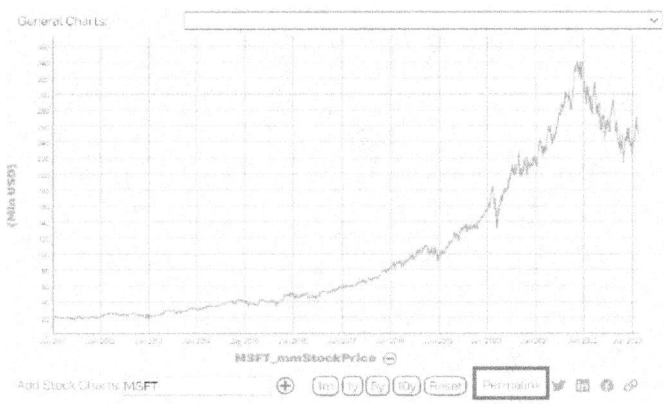

The page that is generated from the script above looks like this:

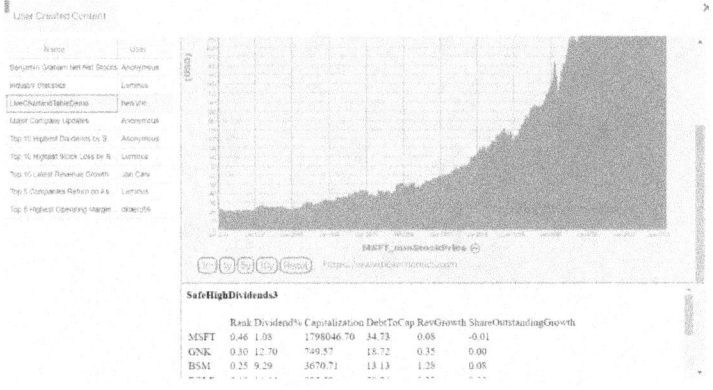

Now you can imagine how powerful the page generated with such scripts can be. Take a look at the script-generated company page below. It is possible to generate very sophisticated and live reports with the Tickernomics scripting engine:

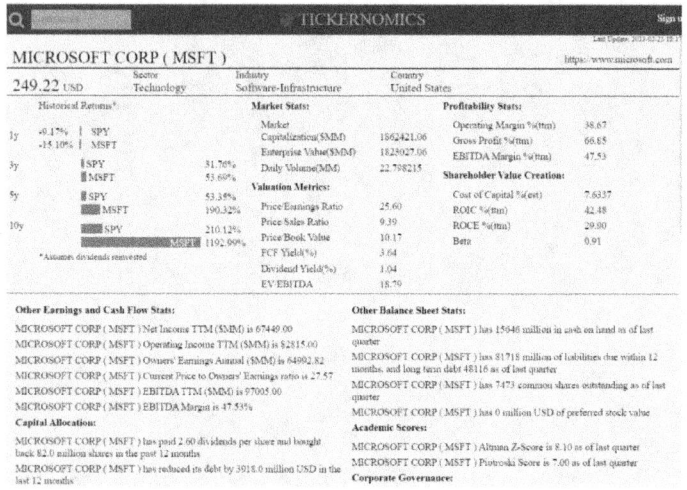

The company lookup at the top of the page was generated using :

```
AddStaticTemplate(pageName,"","companylookup")
```

30
THE END IS JUST THE BEGINNING

This is the final chapter in our journey to become an algorithmic investor. We learned that an unemotional, mathematical approach to investing is the way to go for the most successful investors out there. We learned that the amount of information available today makes it impossible to perform well as an investor without the help of scripting and automated tools. I showed my approach to investing with both stock picking and portfolio management in general.

The most important lesson we learned together is that there is no universal algorithm for successful investing and instead automated tools and scripts should be used to pre-select and prepare the data in a concise form so our human mind can then draw the final conclusions and act on information of a manageable size. The algorithms can only assist us in decision-making, but the final call is on us because our brain is still the most powerful information-processing machine and can outsmart any software in the world.

You might argue that algorithmic investing takes the fun out of investing since you have to deal with algorithms and myriads of numbers. My answer to that is that it is fun for me and many other people. I look at investing as an investigation, only the perpetrator is a good guy. You gather data processing thousands of suspects first and then you fixate on very few leads, learning about their specifics, their relationships, their expenses, and sources of income. You learn their character and how they behave during the bad times. Then when you finally get your primary suspect, you sentence him to the right number of shares. Isn't it exciting? If you can't find fun in this process maybe investing is not for you and you are going to be better with a financial advisor.

The other important point about investing is the ability to be picky. You shouldn't buy the first thing that you like, even after you have objectively measured it. It is especially true for an investor with very few positions. You might be able to afford to be a little bit less picky later when you have 50 positions or so and are well-diversified, but when you have less than 10 positions you need to be picky, really picky. I would only buy a position if not one, not two, but many things lined up just right. It had to not only be good from financial standing, sentiment standing, and prospect, but it also had to be good from a technical analysis point of view and even today's price fluctuation had to be right. I was very picky at the beginning of my portfolio build-up. Surprisingly it was not as good performing as today, most likely due to my lack of experience. So remember that to compensate for your lack of experience you should become really picky in the beginning!

The end of this book is just the beginning for you as an algorithmic investor. I encourage you to automate your investing tasks and build an efficient system for making investing or trading decisions. If it requires a few dozen scripts to be written, then do so. If you feel that you can make better investing decisions with an extra monitor that would show more data to you then buy that extra monitor. If you feel that you perform best after a jog in the morning then only do the investing decisions after doing the jog. If you made an investment mistake then do your homework and learn from that. Do a checklist of improvements to your system so you do not repeat the mistake again. Transform your decision-making into a state-of-the-art machine. Only then do you stand a chance of outperforming the S&P500 year after year.

In this final chapter, we will learn one more script that can help us in finding useful information in a new way. The feature is called – a hallmark. A hallmark is a small indicator that is designed to draw our attention to something noteworthy that happened to a company recently. You can order companies listed by the number of hallmarks on the companies screen:

Ticker	Name	Hallmarks	mrnPS	Industry	mrnBeta	
SLF	SUN LIFE FINANCIAL INC	5	1.41	Insurance-Diversified	0.54	
RDIV	Rovient Sciences Ltd	5	99.74	Biotechnology		
PTEN	PATTERSON UTI ENERGY INC	9	2.89	Oil & Gas Drilling	1.98	
TTGT	TechTarget Inc	9	4.32	Internet Content & Information	1.05	
FBRT	Franklin BSP Realty Trust Inc	8	4.95	REIT-Mortgage		
OSUR	ORASURE TECHNOLOGIES INC	9	1.16	Medical Instruments & Supplies	0.31	
IAG	IAMGOLD CORP	9	0.35	Gold	1.21	
DDI	DoubleDown Interactive Co. Ltd	9	0.05	Electronic Gaming & Multimedia		
MICS	SINGING MACHINE CO INC	9	0.21	Consumer Electronics	-0.24	

The hallmarks show noteworthy recent changes in the company and there are quite a few pre-built hallmarks:

Flag Type	Hallmark	Number
	Assets jumped a lot recently(%)	57.1276
○	Cash/Investments dropped a lot recently(%)	-34.6693
	Debt to Capital jumped a lot recently(%)	115.0537
	Expenses jumped a lot recently(%)	201.3332
	Free Cash Flow jumped a lot recently(%)	172.2461
	Income jumped a lot recently(%)	424.8924
○	Price to Earnings dropped a lot recently(%)	-57.6989
	Revenue jumped a lot recently(%)	174.8539
	Total Debt jumped a lot recently(%)	202.1339

The cool thing is that scripting allows the creation of your own unique hallmarks, so you can be notified of major company changes directly in the companies list screen. Typically a company with a big number of hallmarks undergoes some kind of monumental changes and it automatically draws the attention of an investor. So if you build your hallmarks, then just ordering companies by the number of hallmarks can provide you with a list of companies with significant changes and you can investigate them further. Big money is always made during a change when the investor is able to accurately forecast the future. It is very hard to make a lot of money during calm times.

Let's look at the script that creates a new custom hallmark ("AddHallmark" in Public Scripts):

```
function run()
  local cap=GetXBRLLatest("AAPL","","mmCapitalization")
  if cap > 2000 then
    DeleteHallmark("AAPL","My Hallmark")
    SetHallmarkPropStr("AAPL","Very High Capitalization","Description","Very High Capitalization!")
    SetHallmarkPropStr("AAPL","Very High Capitalization","Icon","fa fa-hand-peace-o")
    SetHallmarkProp("AAPL", "Very High Capitalization", "Number", cap)
    SetHallmarkProp("AAPL", "Very High Capitalization", "Color", 2349235)
    PrintLn("Created Hallmark")
    StoreHallmarks()
  end
end
```

If you look at this code closely we first delete the hallmark with the name "My Hallmark" if such existed before and then we start setting properties for a hallmark for AAPL stock specifically. So each stock can have its unique hallmark. Notice we even specify a custom icon for it "fa fa hand peace". So it will look like this:

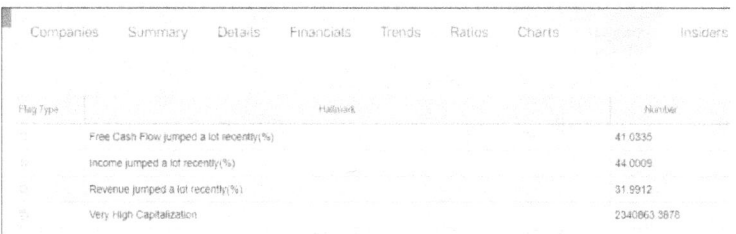

Flag Type	Hallmark	Number
	Free Cash Flow jumped a lot recently(%)	41.0335
	Income jumped a lot recently(%)	44.0009
	Revenue jumped a lot recently(%)	31.9912
	Very High Capitalization	2340863.3878

Finally, we store the hallmark permanently. The number associated with the hallmark here is Apple's capitalization. Think of algorithms you could build that will go in a for-loop through all companies and then you can identify a noteworthy condition so you can create your own hallmark.

You can also iterate over the existing hallmarks and do something about them. So imagine having a script that runs periodically and adds hallmarks and then another script you can use manually or periodically to generate a report similar to the

one below:

Here is the script that generates this report iterating through the hallmarks:

```
local name="Major Company Updates"
ClearStaticPage(name)
ClearStaticPage("Company Hallmarks")
AddToStaticPage(name,"","div","font-size:10px;position:absolute;right:0px;top:0px",
  "Last Update: " .. GetNow())
local idHeader=AddToStaticPage(name,"","div",
  "font-size:20px;height: 4rem;width:100%;display:flex; justify-content:center;",
"Major Company Updates")
local idBody=AddToStaticPage(name,"","div","margin-top:1rem;width:100%;","")
local companylist={}
local companysorting={}
for i=0, GetTickerCount(), 1
do
  local ticker=GetTickerByIndex(i)
  local hallmarkcount=GetHallmarkCount(ticker)
  if(hallmarkcount~=nill) then
    if(hallmarkcount>0) then
      if(hallmarkcount<4) then
        companylist[ticker]=hallmarkcount
        companysorting[ticker]=GetCompanyPropStr(ticker,"Name")
      end
    end
  end
end
local hallmarks = getKeysSortedByValue(companysorting, function(a, b) return a < b end)
for _, key in ipairs(hallmarks) do
  local companyname=GetCompanyPropStr(key, "Name")
  local headertext=companyname .. "(" .. key .. ")"
  PrintLn(headertext)
  local message=""
  local idCompName=AddToStaticPage(name,idBody,"h1",
    "font-size:16px;display:flex; justify-content:center;",headertext)
```

229

```
for i=0, companylist[key], 1 do
  if(i~=companylist[key]) then
    local hallmarkname=GetHallmarkName(key, i)
    local hallmarkproperty=math.abs(math.floor(GetHallmarkProp(key, hallmarkname, "Number")))
    local hallmarkmessage=StringReplace(hallmarkname,"(%)","")
    if message~="" then
      message = message .. " "
    end
    message=message .. companyname .. " " .. hallmarkmessage ..
    " by " .. hallmarkproperty .. " percent."
  end
end
AddToStaticPage(name,idBody,"p",
  "display:flex;justify-content:center;margin-left:3rem; margin-right:3rem",message)
end
```

The script above creates static content that everyone can see, but if you are a private person and want some of the reports to be generated just for you then you can store the data in the Prospects feature via StoreProspect scripting command . It is a Tickernomics notepad-like feature where you can take notes, and insert charts and tables about the companies you are investigating. The scripts can generate your own prospects.

Here is how to create a prospect document (in ProseMirror format):

```
function run()
  StoreProspect("new prospect","no ticker",
  "{\"doc\" :{\"content\" :[{\"content\" : [{\"text\" : \"My test \", \"type\" : \"text\""..
  "},{ \"marks\" :[ {\"type\" : \"strong\"} ],\"text\" : \"prospect!\","..
  "\"type\" : \"text\" }], \"type\" : \"paragraph\"}], \"type\" : \"doc\""..
  "},\"selection\" :{\"anchor\" : 1,\"head\" : 1,\"type\" : \"text\" }}"
  )
end
```

and the result:

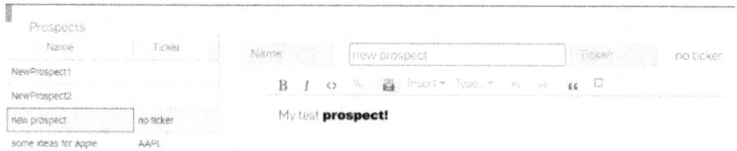

That's it folks! Good luck!